THAILAND

BY
BEN DAVIES

Produced by
Thomas Cook Publishing

Written by Ben Davies
Updated by David Henley

Photography by Rick Strange and David Henley/
CPA Media
Original design by Laburnum Technologies Pvt Ltd

Editing and page layout by Cambridge Publishing
Management Ltd, Unit 2, Burr Elm Court,
Caldecote CB3 7NU
Series Editor: Karen Beaulah

Published by Thomas Cook Publishing
A division of Thomas Cook Tour Operations Ltd

PO Box 227, The Thomas Cook Business Park,
Unit 18, Coningsby Road,
Peterborough PE3 8SB, United Kingdom
E-mail: books@thomascook.com
www.thomascookpublishing.com
Tel: +44 (0) 1733 416477

ISBN-13: 978-1-84157-605-3
ISBN-10: 1-84157-605-0

Project Editor: Diane Ashmore
Production/DTP Editor: Steven Collins

Printed and bound in Spain by: Grafo Industrias Graficas, Basauri.

Cover design by: Liz Lyons Design, Oxford.
Front cover credits: Left © Ifa-Biderteam, Photolibrary.com; centre © Waterfall William,
Pacific Stock, Photolibrary.com; right © Neil Emerson, Robert Harding Pictures, Getty Images
Back cover credits: Left © Neil Emerson, Robert Harding Pictures, Photolibrary.com;
right © Arioshi Rita, Pacific Stock, Photolibrary.com

Contents

KEY TO MAPS

✈ Airport

1835m▲ Mountain

★ Start of walk/tour

• • Ferry route

⌐ Ancient walls

➤ ➤ Detour

(407) Road number

⌐ Rail line

Maps

Walks and Tours

Features

Introduction

Up to 12 hours by plane or four weeks by boat from Europe, but a world away in spirit, the Kingdom of Thailand remains the quintessence of Eastern promise. Thailand is often called the 'Land of Smiles'. With its chequered rice fields, glittering temples and turquoise seas, it exudes a dreamy unreality. Yet with its crowded cities and bustling markets, it reflects the sheer immediacy of a people living life to the full.

Mae Sot, in the far northwest near the Burmese border

Here, packed in a country the size of France, are countless worlds: hill tribes cultivating opium, high-tech industries churning out silicon chips, and more than 60 per cent of the population working the fields much as they have done for centuries.

From the lush countryside and palm-fringed islands to the polluted capital of Bangkok seems like a million miles. But even here, amid the BMWs, the five-star hotels and chaotic side streets, there is little that is conventional, and contrasts abound. What enchants one visitor appals the next, and the unexpected is the only norm.

Who can be indifferent to the sight of a Buddhist monk collecting alms from a layman, or a hill-tribe woman buying kebabs in the market? Who can imagine the exhaust fumes of a million cars, but also the smell of a million flowers and the calm of a *wat* (temple) surrounded by gilded Buddhas?

The country is, however, no longer the undiscovered paradise of yesteryear. But with its 25 million rice farmers, its king, and its religion of compromise, the kingdom still offers visitors the feel of the East tinged with the comforts of the West, along with the excitement, the frustrations and the feel of some place many worlds away. Sometimes colourful, sometimes chaotic, Thailand has, by and large, managed to remain uniquely itself.

'The men are black, the zone is hot and the inhabitants much given to pleasure and ryot.'
SAMUEL PURCHAS, early 17th-century explorer

'It makes you laugh with delight to think that anything so fantastic could exist on this sombre earth. They are gorgeous; they glitter with gold and whitewash, yet are not garish.'
WILLIAM SOMERSET MAUGHAM

'The streets, stretching out of sight, are alleys of clear running water. The horizon is tall trees, above which are visible the sparkling towers and pyramids of the pagodas. Certainly, I myself have never seen lovelier.'
ABBÉ DE CHOISY

'This Kingdom is good. In the water there are fish, in the fields there is rice. The ruler does not levy taxes . . . the faces of the people are happy.'
13th-century stone inscription found in Sukhothai

The spelling of place names used on the maps and within the text of this book has been transcribed from the Thai language; consequently slight variations may occur between these name forms and those used locally.

Wat Phra Kaeo, detail from the royal chapel inside the Grand Palace, Bangkok

One of Thailand's many spectacular beaches at Ko Samet

The jungle-covered peak at Khao Sok National Park

The land

The Kingdom of Thailand lies just south of the Tropic of Cancer, some 9,485km (5,984 miles) from London or Paris and some 7,495km (4,657 miles) from Sydney. It is part of the vast area known as Indo-China which includes the neighbouring countries of Laos, Cambodia and Myanmar.

Formed millions of years ago, the Indo-Chinese land mass was reshaped over the centuries by earthquakes and volcanic activity that created the fairy tale rock formations at Phang Nga, as well as the magnificent limestone ridges of the northern hills.

These same geological processes gave the kingdom its irregular shape, which Thais compare to an elephant's head. To the north is the rounded skull, towards Khorat in the east is the protruding ear. Bangkok is located at the elephant's

mouth. To the south, the trunk extends all the way down to the border with Malaysia.

Undreamt-of variety
Thailand is a delightfully varied country. Parts of its extensive coastline would be the envy of any tropical island paradise, while the coastal plains, rainforests, lush valleys and dramatic mountains only add to the scenic variety.

You will not find snow here, however. Thailand's highest point is only 2,565m (8,415ft) above sea level at Doi Inthanon near Chiang Mai in the north. Though high hills continue down the west part of the country, following the Myanmar (Burmese) border down to the coast of Malaysia, they cannot match their Himalayan parentage.

On the other hand, Thailand does have plains in vast quantity, rich fertile tracts of land that have made the country one of the most productive rice growers in the world – harvesting more than 20 million tonnes every year. These plains are irrigated by the great rivers of Ping, Yom and Nan which snake down from the north to the town of Nakhon Sawan, where they merge to form the great Chao Phraya River, known as the 'Mother of Waters'. The Mekong River cuts through the arid chain of land that lies to the northeast, formed by the Khorat plateau, which extends through the poorest part of the country.

Almost midway down the land mass, the kingdom narrows. The Tenasserim and Phuket hills, an important source of tin, lie down the western coast, leaving room on the east coast for rubber and coconut plantations, and the endless beaches that have become the gems in Thailand's tourist crown.

With 76 provinces and a land mass the size of France, Thailand still manages to come out with some fairly disparate statistics. The distance from the northern to the southern tip is 1,700km (1,056 miles), and from the arid plains of Khorat to the border with Myanmar is 800km (497 miles). South of Bangkok, the land narrows to as little as 16km (10 miles) – so small a distance that on clear days it is possible to look from one coast to the other.

Of the total land mass, 60 per cent is under plantations, mainly rice, rubber and tapioca, products that have made Thailand one of the biggest agricultural producers in the world. A further 20 per cent is under forest, a figure that has fallen rapidly since the days when much of the countryside was a mass of jungle, but which is still enough to conserve vast areas of teak and pine. Even the two coastlines are different, the one green and tropical, the other characterised by hills and limestone formations.

Given this variety, it is hardly surprising that visitors can come back to Thailand year after year, visiting different towns and regions, and each time discover yet another aspect of this fascinating country.

Southwest of Chiang Mai the plains of Doi Suthep are covered by paddy fields

History

3500 BC	Traces of an early Bronze Age civilisation discovered in Ban Chiang, northeast Thailand.	**1279–98**	Reign of King Ramkhamhaeng (Rama the Brave), one of the great early monarchs.
8th–11th century AD	Arrival of the Mons and Khmers from Cambodia.	**1350**	Founding of Ayutthaya.
10th–12th century	Thais migrate from China into northern Thailand, displacing the Khmers.	**1378**	Sukhothai becomes a vassal state of neighbouring Ayutthaya, a powerful Thai kingdom to the south.
1238	Founding of Sukhothai, the first independent Thai kingdom in the period known as the 'Dawn of Happiness'.	**1390–1431**	Ayutthaya expands to include Chiang Mai and parts of Cambodia.
		1600–88	Golden Age of Ayutthaya. The Court receives emissaries from France, Portugal, Holland and Britain.
		1656–88	Reign of King Narai. Thai ambassadors sent to the Court of Louis XIV.
		1767	Conquest and destruction of Ayutthaya by the Burmese. All but

Three of Thailands revered monarchs: Taksin (left), Rama VI (right), and Rama VIII (far right)

10,000 of the inhabitants are killed or taken into slavery and the city is laid to waste.

1768	King Taksin drives out the Burmese and moves the capital to Thonburi.
1782	Taksin goes insane and is executed by being beaten to death with a scented sandalwood club.
1782–1809	Reign of Rama I, the first king of the great Chakri dynasty. A new capital is declared in Bangkok.
1809–24	Reign of Rama II.
1824–51	Reign of Rama III, the king renowned for embracing Buddhism.
1851–68	Reign of Rama IV, known as King Mongkut, one of the great reformers of the 19th century and the ruler depicted in the film *The King and I*.
1855–8	Trade treaties signed with Britain, France and the United States.
1868–1910	Reign of Rama V, known as King Chulalongkorn, the man credited with bringing Thailand into the modern world.
1910–25	Reign of Oxford-educated Rama VI, known as King Vajiravudh.
1925	Beginning of the reign of Eton-educated Rama VII, known as King Prajadhi-pok.
1932	First in a long line of coups by the military. Rama VII steps aside and a constitutional monarchy is declared.
1935–46	Reign of Rama VIII, the child king who was mysteriously found shot in bed. The enigma of the death has yet to be solved.
1941	Japanese occupation of Thailand with the compliance of the Thai government. Opposition groups operate underground.

1946	Reign of Rama IX, known as King Bhumiphol Adulyadej, best loved of the Chakri monarchs, begins.
1965	The Thais remain ostensibly neutral in the Vietnam war but allow US bases on Thai soil.
1973	Students protest in Bangkok against the military. More than 200 are killed or wounded.
1976	A further coup sparked off by a violent confrontation between police and students. The army seizes control.
1981	Abortive coup attempt by army officers known as the 'Young Turks'.
1988	Advent of democratically elected government and the beginning of an economic boom.
1991	The 17th coup brings the Chatichai administration to an end on the grounds of corruption.
1991–2	Military caretaker government, under Prime Minister Anand.
March 1992	General Suchinda appointed Prime Minister.
May 1992	Pro-democracy protestors shot down by troops in Bangkok.
September 1992	Democracy survives under Chuan Leekpai's long-lasting government.
July 1995	Chart Thai party is elected amid growing cynicism about political corruption.
1996	50th anniversary of King Bhumiphol's reign. New Aspiration Party elected, led by Chavalit Yongchaiyudh.
1997	Effects of the late 1990s Asian economic crisis. Democratic Party leader Chuan Leekpai is given another chance before the economic collapse.
2001	Billionaire business tycoon Thaksin Shinawatra's 'Thai Rak Thai' party sweeps to power for the first time.
2004	Under Thaksin's guidance the economy improves markedly and he is re-elected.
2006	Southeast Asia's largest airport, Suvarnabhumi International Airport, opens after many years of delays.

King Chulalongkorn
Rama V is perhaps
Thailand's greatest king

Governance

The history of Thailand has been characterised by political change. Seventeen coups have shaped the face of the kingdom, while more than 20 constitutions and prime ministers have shown the vulnerability of the political game and the enduring power of the military. Despite this, until the early 20th century, politics was an irrelevance, and the monarchy the all-pervading power. For the four centuries prior to that, subjects who even so much as looked at the monarch could have had their heads chopped off.

Although change began with the great Chakri kings – and especially with Rama V (1868–1910), who ended the ancient custom of prostration – the real death knell only came in 1932, when the military took power and absolute monarchy was abolished. Since then, the pendulum has swung from the military to democracy and back again.

Yet, for all the turbulence and the colourful rhetoric, Thailand has managed to avoid the civil wars that have torn neighbouring Cambodia, Laos and Vietnam apart, and in so doing has, paradoxically, established itself as one of the most stable and loyal members of the non-communist world as well as a leading voice in ASEAN, the Association of South East Asian Nations.

The decades of unrest

The first military coup of 1932 brought an end to absolute monarchy, changing

A typical provincial government
building at
Lamphun

Monument to democracy in Bangkok

Taste of democracy

Today, democracy is no longer a strange word to the Thais. It has started to give a voice to the nation, a vote to the people. Tighter controls by the legislative council have lead to a reduction in vote buying. The year 2001 saw many 'power-hungry' politicians disqualified. Since the formation of the 'Thai Rak Thai' party, the average person is tending to pay more attention to local politics than ever before. Only time will tell if this change will last.

the pattern of politics for good and ushering in a period of uncertainty.

During subsequent decades, Thailand withstood the winds of change that were reshaping Indo-China, but the Vietnam War, and the consequent influx of Americans, once again led to the declaration of martial law. When students took to the streets in the 1970s to demonstrate against the military, tanks were sent in and hundreds of students were killed or wounded. In the aftermath, the military leaders were forced to step down. A new coalition government took power, and for a period of three years, the status quo remained intact. Since then, the political theatricals have continued, although, with the exception of the early 1990s, violence has been almost entirely absent.

It is little surprise that the Thais regard the whole business of politics with humour. The constant flux keeps people intrigued, but rarely does it change things. Bangkok residents complain that the wrong government gets in whoever they vote for. To foreigners this is a sign of instability, but to the Thais it is just a sign of life and a reflection of the nature of people themselves.

The old National Assembly Hall, Bangkok

Constitutionally, however, the country is governed by a cabinet and a national assembly, supported by a highly educated civil service. Moving down the parliamentary pyramid are the 76 provinces, each with a governor and a provincial capital. And at the bottom, there are hundreds of thousands of village councils.

For all that, control of the purse strings, and the people, means that the military is never far from power. They still have their own investment funds, their own political alliances, even their own bank.

However, that position may change as the country rebuilds itself after the 1997 economic collapse and the threat of communism – and the fear of Vietnam, Myanmar and Laos – is finally laid to rest. But as the 1992 brutal suppression of pro-democracy protestors has demonstrated, the military remains a critical force – and politics, an unpredictable and, for a large number of Thais, a largely irrelevant matter.

Culture

All the colour and all the exotic arts of the East are to be found in Thailand. Whether classical dancing, an arrangement of jasmine flowers or a temple mural, the country excels in its artistic achievements. Nor is this merely a show of Eastern convention, but one of the clearest examples of the people's love of colour and of life.

Playing traditional instruments at a folk fair

The most famous monument in all Thailand, the Grand Palace in Bangkok, with its clutch of gilded and glistening spires, its murals of the Ramayana, and the revered temple of the Emerald Buddha, is in many ways the quintessential Thai edifice. But if you miss the Grand Palace there are plenty of other examples. Indeed, some estimates put the number of temples at 26,000 and Buddha images at 5 million, about 1 for every 12 people of the Kingdom.

The invisible force

Buddhism is all pervasive in Thailand. The 'middle way' is the religion of 95 per cent of the people. Buddhism came from India 2,300 years ago, brought by missionaries from the Emperor Ashoka. It has influenced not only the people, but also the art that they have produced. Paintings and Buddhist *tankhas* and exquisite wooden and stone statues of the Buddhas, old and new, can be found in markets around the country.

Early religious writings provided strict rules for creating any image of the Buddha. They were to have 32 primary features and 80 secondary ones. Even so, Thai artists left their own indelible

marks as a reflection of the age in which they lived. Early styles show the broad, rugged features of the Buddha with bulging eyes, often in the position of subduing Mara, the symbol of all evil.

During the 13th and 14th centuries, the Buddhas became more serene, the features less pronounced, culminating in the famous Sukhothai Buddha, the high point of Thai art. Later periods could not match such artistic heights and the art of the Bangkok period (late 17th century onwards) degenerated into the production of ornate, heavy-handed royal figures.

Various other influences have also moulded the kingdom throughout its history, including Indian mythology and the art of the early Khmer and Mon civilisations. These too have been absorbed and reworked into something unique and quintessentially Thai.

A wealth of wats

A *wat* is a temple (*see pp46–7*), but it is also a communal home for monks, a gathering point for the village, and, traditionally, even a school. Originally they were simple structures made of wood and found in every rural commune. Later, *wats* were built specifically to contain relics of the Buddha himself. The most important *wats* are called *pra that* or *wat mahathat,* and are supported by royalty. Others are funded by the people themselves who give money in order to win merit and secure themselves a better life in the next earthly cycle.

Going for a song

Music to the Thais is as sweet as to the Western ear. Thai classical music uses different notes to those of the Western scale. It originally accompanied dances and played for royalty. In later years, classical music found its way into local festivals where a *piphat* orchestra, comprising 15 to 20 members, banged

gongs called *gong wong yai,* or played the Thai xylophone known as the *ranad.*

These days, the place to hear classical music is in tourist restaurants or, if you are lucky, the National Theatre. Do not expect to hear it outside these establishments. Thai and international pop music now takes precedence, and that is what you are likely to hear everywhere throughout the country.

Wat Phra Kaeo, in the Grand Palace, Bangkok, is the most dazzling of all Thailand's glittering temples

Festivals

Countless festivals take place during the Thai year, giving visitors a chance to share these delightful national occasions. Some festivals are local, others national. Whatever they celebrate, the festivities are almost always accompanied by feasts and by dancing, by beauty contests, and by unbridled merrymaking. Dates vary from year to year, so always check with offices of the Tourism Authority of Thailand (TAT).

People at the Visakha Puja Festival, Bangkok

Chiang Mai Flower Festival
First weekend in February
Beautiful flower parades and processions held when the northern flowers are in full bloom.

Magha Puja
End of February, all Thailand
One of the most important Buddhist holidays, held to commemorate the occasion when 1,250 disciples gathered spontaneously to hear the Master preach. Throughout the country, candle-lit processions are held around temples.

Poi Sang Long
Beginning April, Mae Hong Son, Chiang Mai and northern Thailand
Three days of colourful processions to celebrate the ordination of novices progressing to full monkhood.

Pattaya Festival
In April, 19th onwards, Pattaya
Celebration with beer, floats, beauty contests, and all the other things that the resort is known for.

Songkran
12–14 April particularly at Chiang Mai
The traditional Thai New Year and one of the great annual festivities. People sprinkle water over monks, cover Buddha images with fresh flowers, clean their houses in a symbolic gesture of renewal, and fling water everywhere in celebration.

The Ploughing Ceremony
Early May, Bangkok
Sacred bulls are offered a variety of grains. Depending on what they eat, seers will forecast the rice crop for the year. You will have to obtain tickets beforehand at the Tourism Authority of Thailand (TAT) office on Ratchadaphisek Road (*tel: 0 2694 1222*).

Visakha Puja
End May, all Thailand
The most sacred of all Buddhist days, commemorating Buddha's birth, enlightenment and death. Beautiful candle-lit processions are held outside the temples.

International Swan-Boat Races
September, Chao Phraya River
Traditional swan-boat racing held
on the Chao Phraya River under
Bangkok's Rama IX Bridge.

Phuket Vegetarian Festival
October
A 10-day festival in which many of the
island's Chinese residents perform
extraordinary feats, walking on red-hot
coals and piercing their skin with spikes,
in an effort to cleanse their spirit.

Chon Buri Buffalo Races
Mid-October
Buffaloes are let loose around a track
with much betting and local merriment.

Loi Krathong
Late October/November, all Thailand
The most beautiful of all the Thai
festivals. People from all over the
kingdom make little boats from banana
leaves, place a candle and a joss stick
inside, and launch them on to the rivers
and canals in a blaze of colour. The best

place to celebrate is Sukhothai or
Chiang Mai.

Surin Elephant Round-Up
Third week November
A celebration of Thailand's most
famous beast. Displays of elephant
football, tug-of-war and even boxing.
Arrange accommodation well ahead.

River Khwae Bridge Week
Late November/early December
Light and Sound shows and handicraft
displays to recall the destruction of
the bridge and the so-called 'Death
Railway' during World War II.

Trooping of the Colours
3 December, Bangkok
Colourful royal regiments pass before
the King on the Royal Plaza in front of
the old National Assembly building.

King's Birthday
5 December, all Thailand
Processions held throughout the
kingdom to celebrate the King's birthday.

Floating *krathong* on a river, Loy Krathong Festival

Impressions

Everyone visiting Thailand is struck by the relative ease of getting around, and the openness of the people with whom they come into contact. Trains run on time, white towels are offered for mopping your brows, and the tourist police speak English (most of the time) and smile. Thais are known for their good manners.

The traditional *wai* or Thai greeting

The initial impression of Westernisation is almost misleading. Like any Asian country, Thailand has its own unique customs; while many are merely a matter of courtesy, others are so deep-set that they fill the visitor with wonder. It is no coincidence that the Thais call Westerners *farangs* (foreigners). Below is a checklist of things to remember. Thais are tolerant people, but it is best to try and fit in.

Thailand

Culture shock

If your first stop is Bangkok, prepare for that experience known as culture shock which is commonly made up of heat, lead pollution and dismay. To survive the maelstrom on the senses, reduce initial hassles to a minimum: make sure you have a hotel reservation, take a metered taxi from the airport, buy a map, and refuse all touts.

If you are arriving after a long-haul flight, take things slowly to begin with. Drink lots of water and go easy on sunbathing. Most doctors advise sleep. Better still, find a spot near the river to sit and absorb the calm and the chaos.

The next day get up early, before the traffic, and explore the sights and sounds. Leave your preconceived notions behind. Remember that the Thai religion of impermanence negates the need to hurry. In Thailand life goes at its own speed: in Bangkok at a chaotic rate, and in the rice fields and government offices at a slow ebb. Nothing a tourist can do will change that. The only way to handle it is to be as the Buddhists, and accept.

Entering the spirit of the place

Thais are a fun-loving race. As such, they want everyone else to have fun when they are in Thailand. To join the party you generally do not have to go far. People come up to talk to you or to drink with you. Often, they want to know about your family, whether you are married and how much you earn.

Do not be offended by such questions. You can be evasive if you do not want to answer them. Always beware of those who try to befriend you for other reasons. There are always some individuals who prey on tourists for what they can get – be it free meals or money for tours. Treat people with courtesy, but never lower your guard completely.

Greetings

The traditional Thai greeting, known as the *wai*, is a gracefully fluent movement that is still commonly used. Hold the palms of your hands together and bring them up to your chin. Bend forward, lowering the head. Traditionally, the more important the person, the lower you bend. Thais generally greet one another thus, but they greet foreigners with handshakes. Even so, it can do no harm to learn the Thai way.

Linguistic nuances

Thai is a complex language. It is tonal, and has 44 consonants and 38 vowels. Given time constraints, most visitors get little opportunity to practise speaking the language. For those who would like to try, however, it is still worth investing a few hours prior to departure in learning a few of the essentials. On the positive side, there are no changes for tense, gender or plurals so the grammar is easy.

Try, with the help of a phrase book, to master a few basic words. Remember that at the end of every phrase, males say *krap* and females say *ka*. The Thais are extremely polite and any attempt at learning their language will be greatly appreciated.

Making offerings at the Erawan shrine, Bangkok

Northern Thailand

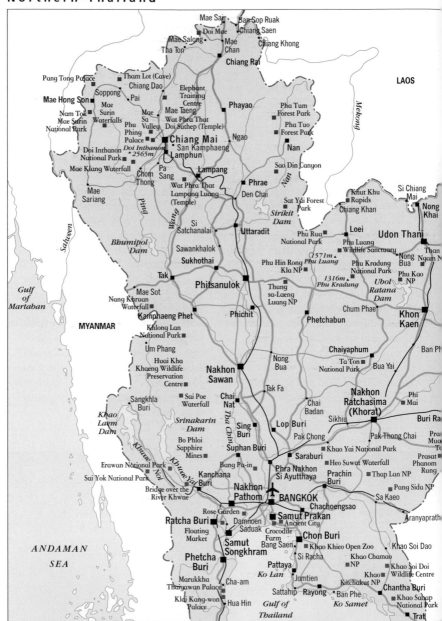

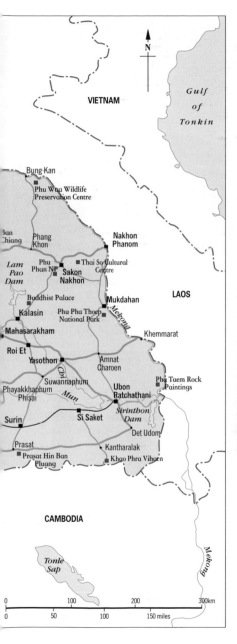

The proverbial smile

The Thai smile: there is no other hallmark that is quite so endemic. But like many such 'Thaisms', it can conceal a host of meanings. Thais smile because they are happy. They smile because they are embarrassed. Some smile because it makes them money. Accept their smiles and try to reciprocate, but never jump to conclusions about their meaning.

In the same way, Thais rarely show anger. When they do, it is with uncharacteristic vigour. Never argue excessively, and if you are angry, smile and leave. The Thais themselves do this all the time and, for the most part, it seems to work.

The Thai smile, Rayong-style

The spirits

On top of almost every post, or situated outside almost any building, you will find a miniature house or temple known as the *chao thai*. This normally contains joss sticks, rice and water; it often has beds and accommodates the single most important resident of the house: the *phra phum* or lord

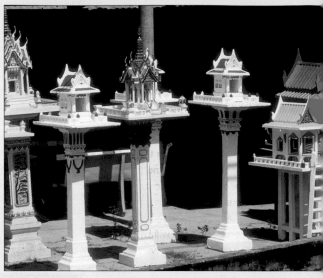

of the place. Here people make daily offerings of food, flowers, incense and candles.

Spirits not only live in the towns and cities of Thailand, but also in the trees, in the hills, in the winds and in the rain.

They are believed to be the biggest determinants of good fortune, and, if not treated properly and with the proper deference due to them, the reason for bad luck. You should never whistle at night, as Thais believe this will call spirits out and haunt you!

Farmers hoping for a good harvest, young girls looking for a suitable husband, or gamblers hoping to win a lottery: none can afford to ignore them. When a new office block is to be built, the spirit house will be the first thing to be planned. And when a tree is cut down, a special ceremony will be held to appease the misplaced spirit within. The most famous spirit house was erected as a result of many deaths during the construction of a hotel. Known as the Erawan shrine on Radjadamri Road, it is one of the most revered shrines in Thailand.

In the far north of the country, many of the tribespeople hold offerings to the 'grandmother of the crops'; while in the south, local fishermen erect phalluses pointing out to sea to fertilise the water. Not all Thais believe everything they are told about spirits. However, being a practical people, and just as there is some basis to an old belief, almost everyone will make offerings in the hope that it will do them good.

Appeasing the spirits: Facing page: spirit houses come in all shapes and sizes, as do the offerings placed in them. This page below: a woman makes a floral offering

Purchasing power

Unless in doubt, bargain. That is the golden rule. It applies in shops, in markets, in non-metered taxis, and occasionally even with travel agents. The art of bargaining is to decide how much you are prepared to pay for a given product or service beforehand, and if possible to get it cheaper.

This is the way it works: you see a lurid green lacquerware pot which you can imagine in your home. Ask how much it is (*taorai?* in Thai). The salesman will quote you a price 30 to 50 per cent too high. You must say 'too expensive' (*peng pai*), and quote a price 20 per cent lower than you believe the pot is worth. The salesman will then, in all likelihood, lower his original price and you, in turn, should increase yours, but never above your original target. At this point, the salesman may well tell you that he cannot make money, that he has 20 children to feed and a blind mother-in-law. Smile, but look unimpressed, finger through some different articles and put in a final offer. If he accepts, you are obliged to pay up: if not, move on and start again.

If you cannot speak Thai, use each finger to denote 10 baht. Most shops now use calculators, keying in their own price, then allowing you to put in yours before coming out with a compromise.

Tackling the touts

From the moment you arrive in Thailand, you will become the object of adulation for a strange breed of individual known as the tout. Touts dress smartly, generally speak good English, and make their money by

Monks walk everywhere, as personal motorised transport is forbidden

persuading you to go on special tours, by acting as your private guide, and by taking you on shopping trips.

You are strongly advised to resist their attentions. Touts are outlawed. They may be friendly but could cost you an arm and a leg. If you are in doubt, ask for advice at your hotel or at the tourist office. Official tour guides all carry official Tourism Authority of Thailand (TAT) identity cards.

Taxis and tuk tuks

One of the first things you will be confronted with on arrival is a three-wheeled, unsightly, smelly motorbike taxi. This contraption is known as a *tuk tuk*. It is Thailand's favourite and fastest means of city transport. *Tuk tuks* are relatively cheap, are available at almost any hour, and are generally safe.

To get a *tuk tuk* all you need to do is wave one down. Tell the driver where you want to go, and agree a price before you get in (you must bargain).

Bangkok and the main cities also offer an abundance of conventional metered and non-metered taxis, *songthaews* (pick-up trucks) and three-wheeled pedal cycles. Whichever mode of transport you take, make sure you fix a price before you leave (*see* Local Transport *on p187*).

The three pillars

In the Thai mentality, three bastions rise above all others: the King, Buddhism and the Nation. Never speak against them or question them unduly.

Monks, especially, should be regarded as sacrosanct. Women should not touch them, nor pass anything directly to them. Especial care should be taken on crowded buses. Similarly, never take liberties when talking about the royal family. Even today, despite tremendous strides towards Westernisation and the gradual erosion of certain values (for example, you often see monks smoking), the people take a fiercely patriotic line.

What to wear

Thais dress neatly. Whether rich or poor, from the city or the country, they take great pains on how they present themselves, believing that appearance reflects status. Foreigners are not expected to follow suit, but they are expected to show a little respect. Topless sunbathing is widespread on almost all the main tourist beaches, but it is still widely looked down upon by the local inhabitants. Jackets and ties may not be common requirements, but in the really exclusive hotel restaurants they are appreciated and, sometimes, required.

When visiting *wats* (temples), make sure that you look presentable (no shorts or sleeveless tops should be worn). And when entering people's homes, always remember to take off your shoes.

A tourist poses with girls in national dress

EXPLORING THE COUNTRYSIDE

Once you have got your feet firmly on Thai soil, the next step is to organise an itinerary. This is the easiest part. Thailand has a vast choice of sights and countless tour agencies to arrange your visits to them.

Most visitors will want to spend a few days in the capital, Bangkok, exploring the markets, canals and temples. During this time you can acclimatise, book tickets, and arrange the remainder of your holiday.

Many destinations are now accessible by air, others by train and bus. Do not, however, make the mistake of trying to fit everything into a two-week trip. Air travel may make the trip physically possible, but delays and hassles will make it more trouble than it is worth.

The mountainous north

The north is where the mountains and hill tribes are to be found. This is the most popular region for visitors, with Chiang Mai – the capital – playing host to top-class hotels and endless numbers of guest houses. People come here to go trekking or to explore the 'Golden Triangle' and the delightful charms of Lanna, the old Thai kingdom that flourished centuries ago.

The arid plains of the northeast

The northeast is an area of vast arid plains stretching to the Cambodian and Laotian borders. Increased interest in this area has led to many new tours being organised, as the region contains beautiful old Khmer ruins, and retains the feel of traditional Thailand, with its plodding water buffalo and poor rural

Khmer ruins in northeastern Thailand

communities. Isaan, the Thai name for this region, is for those who want to get away from it all, who have more time and fewer expectations, and who, preferably, speak a few words of the language. Sights are a considerable distance apart and are mainly situated out of town. Private transport is a definite advantage.

The Gulf of Thailand

The strip of land known as the Gulf (southeast of Bangkok) offers the closest beaches to the capital. Originally, it sprang up around Pattaya, but it now extends all the way from Bang Saen to Rayong. For those who have less time or who want a weekend break, it has good swimming as well as the beautiful island of Ko Samet: further afield is Ko Chang island and the inland Southern Beaches.

For those in search of beaches and islands, the south is the region to come to. It comprises some 2,080km (1,292 miles) of coastline, washed by balmy seas, as well as coral reefs and delicious seafoods. Some islands – like Phuket and Ko Samui – have become international destinations with five-star hotels. Others, like Krabi, offer a taste of relatively unspoilt beach paradise with a variety of accommodation.

Southern Thailand

CAMBODIA

Nakhon Pathom
BANGKOK
Rose Garden
Ratcha Buri
Damnoen
Saduak
Samut Prakan
Ancient City
Crocodile Farm
Floating Market
Bang
Samut Songkhram
Saen
Chon Buri
Bight
Khao Khieo
of
Open Zoo
Khao
Khao Soi Dao
Phetcha
Buri
Bangkok
Si Racha
Chamao
Khao Soi Doi
N P
Wildlife Centre
Marukkha
Cha-am
Ko Lan
Pattaya
Jomtien
Rayong
Khao Kitchakut
Thaiyawan Palace
Sattahip
Ban Phe
N P
Klai Kang-won Palace
Hua Hin
Chantha Buri
Khao Sabap
Ko
N P
Samet
Laem Ngop
Trat

MYANMAR
Kui Buri
Prachuap
Khiri Khan
Ko Chang
Gulf
Ko Mak
of
Ko Kut
Thap Sakae
Thailand
Bang Saphan

ANDAMAN
Pathiu
SEA
Chumphon

Sawi
Ko Tao
Ang Thong
Ko Chang
Ranong
Marine N P
La Mae
Na
Ko Phangan
Ko Surin
Thon
Nua
Laem Son
Chaiya
Ko Samui
Ko Surin
N P
Don Sak
Tai
Chieo Lan
Khanom
N
Dam
Takuapa
Surat Thani
Khao Sok
Khao Luang
Ko Similan
National Park
National Park
Phang
Nga
1835m ▲
Nakhon
Thai Muang
Than Bokkharam
Si Thammarat
Botanical Gardens
Surin Beach
Krabi
Khao
Thung Song
Hua Sai
Ko Phuket
Ko Yao Yai
Phanom
Patong Beach
Phuket
Bencha NP
Thale Noi
Kata Beach
Ko
Bird Sanctuary
Marine
Phi
Khao
Biological
Phi
Ko
Chong NP
Phatthalung
Research
Don
Lanta
Trang
Khu Khut
Centre &
Ko Ngai
Khlong
Waterbird Park
Aquarium
Ko Libong
Kantang
Lamchan
Thung Wa
Waterbird
Songkhla
Langu
Park
Hat Yai
Ban Pak Bara
Thale Ban
Pattani
Ko Tarutao
N P
Sai Buri
Tarutao Marine
Na Thawi
Yala
N P
Satun
Nam Tok Sai Khao
Narathiwat
Forest Park
Thaksin Rachaniwet
Palace
Than To
Banglang
Ban Taba
Dam
Sungai
Kolok
Betong
MALAYSIA

0   100   200km
0   50   100 miles

Bangkok

With its golden temples, endless traffic jams, and colourful canals, Bangkok is like no other city in Asia. It has around 10 million inhabitants, over 400 temples, and more than 3 million vehicles. You will either love or hate it, but you should not miss it.

The spires of the Royal Palace, across the Chao Phraya from Wat Arun

King Rama I established his capital on the banks of the Chao Phraya River in 1782, shortly after the fall of Ayutthaya. At the time it was little more than a fishing village, but the king built palaces and canals, parks for his elephants and statues of Buddha.

Successive monarchs added further royal residences, tree-lined malls and great temples, pushing the resident Chinese further out of the centre and extending the city on both sides of the Chao Phraya. The Victorians knew it as the 'Venice of the East'.

Much has changed in the intervening period. Since the 1970s, especially, the city has undergone a massive economic boom; canals have been filled in to make way for roads, and high-rises have been built to accommodate the massive influx of people from the provinces. Yet the temples remain, along with many of the waterways, and all the charms and excesses of one of Southeast Asia's last great oriental cities.

The best sights

Bangkok is not an easy place to explore, but effort is appropriately rewarded. If time is short, the Grand Palace, the canals at Thonburi and the temple of Wat Arun should not be missed. These are to Bangkok what the Eiffel Tower is to Paris and the Houses of Parliament to London. Other temples, crowded markets, and statues made of huge quantities of gold are strewn around the city, rewarding those with greater time to explore.

One other experience that no visitor should miss is a morning's shopping, for Bangkok is one of the most exotic and cheapest purchasing centres in the East. The opportunity to try some of the best and spiciest Thai food is yet another key feature. Evening is the time to visit the bars, the discos, or the masseuses for which the metropolis is justifiably renowned.

Many visitors find the easiest way to get around the city is by organised tour. That way, at least you will be spared the problem of negotiating the labyrinthine side streets and crowded buses. Tours will show you all the best-known landmarks, without the heat and exhaust fumes. Most tours include lunch at a Thai restaurant and almost always drop you off at your hotel.

Ultimately, however, the real Bangkok is something felt, not seen, something best explored by yourself with time on your hands, and with endless reserves of patience.

A special energy

Bangkok has a special energy about it, a frenzied chaos that you will find in few other places around the world, but there can also be a genuine calm about it. Vast traffic jams line the streets off Silom Road while, nearby, girls sell orchids by the river. Then there are the special smells, the wafting of kebabs, the car fumes, the markets, the smiles; whimsical, loud, calm. One minute you can be breathing in the exhaust of a thousand revving vehicles, and the next, emerge in the calm of Lumphini Park, or surrounded by the old-worldly grandeur of Jim Thompson's House.

Indeed, the city is only playing out the true meaning of its name (the longest recorded in the *Guinness Book of Records*). Rama I called his capital 'Great City of Angels, the supreme repository of divine jewels, the great land unconquerable, the grand and prominent realm, the royal and delightful capital city full of nine noble gems, the highest royal dwelling and grand palace, the divine shelter and dwelling of the reincarnated spirits.'

Wherever you go and whatever you do, Bangkok will build on that description. It is an assault on the senses and the expectations, a melding of the old and the new and, more than anything, it is a reflection of the Thais themselves: colourful, vibrant and, at the last count, enigmatic.

Bangkok skyline near the World Trade Centre

Bangkok

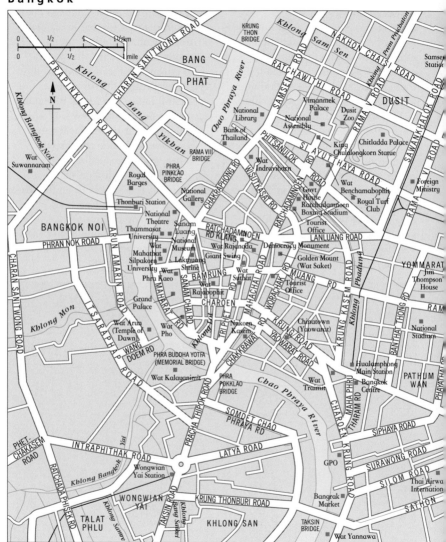

Vimanmek Palace (Cloud Mansion)

Built by King Chulalongkorn in 1901, Vimanmek claims to be the world's largest teak-wood building and stands by a lake in spacious grounds. Chulalongkorn lived here for only a few years but, under the patronage of Queen Sirikit, the building has been restored to its former glory. Inside is an impressive

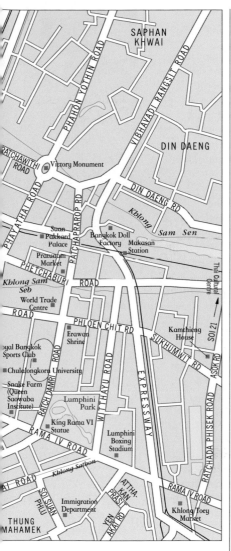

to provide sufficient water for the royal dowse. Vimanmek is surrounded by water on all sides, including the Channel of Fragrant Wood Canal, the Sheet of Glass Canal, the Channel of Silver, and – best known of all – the Jade Basin, named after the water's greenness. *Diagonally opposite the Dusit Zoo, behind the handsome old National Assembly building. Open: daily 9.30am–4pm. Admission charge (Grand Palace ticket allows entry).*

Lead and luxury

It starts at 6.30am: wave after wave of vehicles, motorbikes, packed BTS trains and *tuk tuks* streaming into the city. Lead pollutes the sky, pollutes the roads, and gets into the very soul of the place known as Krungthep, the 'City of Angels'. Bangkok has increasingly more traffic, worse pollution, more people, and it is growing faster than ever in its history.

A number of the many migrants to the city scrape a living selling drinks or plates of noodles; transforming great areas of the city into small villages where they keep chickens and run food stalls. Others work as labourers on building sites. For all, it is the city of hopes, where dreams can come true.

collection of paintings, objets d'art and royal jewellery, as well as the royal bathroom equipped with a shower – believed to be the first ever installed in Thailand. The tank was manually filled

Vimanmek Palace, Bangkok

China Town

Originally the Chinese lived up near the Grand Palace, but they were moved by Rama I to make way for the royal residences. However, the Chinese continue to occupy the most colourful and frenetic part of the city, made up of a labyrinth of narrow streets, wooden houses and crowded lanes. Here you will find small shrines, a gold exchange and a profusion of markets selling exotic remedies for acne and infertility, as well as powdered wigs and sharks' fin soup. Be prepared for crowds.

For a glimpse of the most colourful quarters, wander down one of the side streets off Yaowarat Road. It is so busy you will not want transport (*see also pp34–5*).
Between Charoen Krung (New Rd) & Yaowarat Rd.

Dusit Zoo

The Dusit Zoo contains the capital's biggest collection of wildlife. Inmates include elephants, rhinos and gibbons as well as a variety of exotic birdlife, plants, a komodo dragon and several dozen crocodiles. Children will be thrilled by the snack stores and the paddle boats.

Nearby are the Dusit Palace and the Chitladda Palace, the present residence of the royal family (closed to the public).
Rama V Rd. Open: daily 8am–6pm. Admission charge.

Erawan Shrine

Shrines in Bangkok are as numerous as houses, but the Erawan Shrine is the city's most popular spirit house. It was constructed after a stream of mishaps struck the nearby Erawan Hotel, including the sinking of a boat carrying marble from India. Since proving its effectiveness (there have been no further untoward incidents), the Erawan Shrine has become a popular spot with supplicants from around the city, who come to donate wooden elephants (and occasionally even boiled eggs). The really devout hire dancers to make merit on their behalf.
Ask for the Grand Hyatt Erawan Hotel on Ratchadamri Rd, which is next door. Open: daily 7am–11pm. Free admission.

DISORIENTING YOURSELF

Roads in Bangkok are not always what they seem. Some have three names, others just a number. The situation reflects the lack of city planning. There are, however, several points to remember. Turnings off the main roads are almost invariably called *sois* (lanes or alleys). Each has a number and all the odd-numbered *sois* are located on one side of the road, the even-numbered *sois* on the other. Almost all addresses include both the house number and the *sois* number. One without the other is unusable. To make certain where you are going, check on a map, get a telephone number along with it if possible, and instructions written in Thai. Most hotels will be able to help you.

Giant Swing

Facing the giant *bot* (chapel) of Wat Suthat is the incongruous red swing known as the Sao Ching Cha or Giant Swing. This was originally used for a Brahmin ceremony, held once a year, in which Shiva and Vishnu were supposed to visit the temple. Teams would swing higher and higher in their effort to clutch a bag of money with their teeth. Since several participants were seriously injured when they fell off, the spectacle was abolished.

The Giant Swing is in a square at the end of Bamrung Muang Rd, open 24 hrs daily. Wat Suthat Temple open: 8.30am–8.30pm. Free admission.

Boys playing football near the Giant Swing

A small Chinese shrine in Chinatown, Bangkok

Walk: Around Bangkok's China Town

One of Bangkok's busiest market areas, home to some of the city's most congested streets and numerous sprawling wooden houses.
Allow 2 hours.

Start at Tha Ratchawong Pier (easily reached by express boat). Take the nearest exit and walk down the long wide strip known as Ratchawong Rd which heads due north.

1 Ratchawong Road

Although no longer the strict preserve of the Chinese, Ratchawong remains very much their traditional heartland, with its old banks, trading branches, and shuttered wooden houses. To the right

and left are little alleyways selling hardware and textiles. Some stalls even sell bird's nest soup, believed to boost longevity and libido.

Walk along Ratchawong Rd for 450m (1,476ft) and take the small road to your right signposted Soi Wanit 1, formerly known as Sampeng Lane.

2 Sampeng Lane

Once a maze of alleys containing opium dens and gambling parlours, the famous Sampeng Lane has mellowed in recent years but remains one of the most fascinating and congested areas of the city. Many little side streets specialise in lanterns, others in herbal remedies, fabrics, toys and shoes. Watch out, too, for the little *kong tek* shops where houses and cars made of paper are burnt by the Chinese in order to send them to the spirit world of deceased relatives.

Continue down Soi Wanit 1 until you reach the first main intersection, with Soi Mangkorn, where you will see the old Gold Exchange.

3 Gold Exchange

Of all the buildings along Sampeng Lane, this is one of the most distinguished, with its lovely old façade, its shabby balconies, and its faded air of grandeur. At one time this was the centre for all gold trading. Today, like many shops in China Town, it continues to stock gold bracelets and earrings, carefully weighed out on an ancient pair of scales.

Continue along Soi Wanit 1, past the Gold Exchange; at the next crossing turn left down Issaranuphap Lane, then first right down a small alley into Talaht Kao.

4 Talaht Kao (Old Market)

You can smell Talaht Kao before you ever see it – a nauseous odour of dried fish, squid and prawns piled up in great wicker baskets along the alleyway. This is one of the oldest and most pungent of Bangkok's Chinese markets, but it is strictly for the curious. Purchasers eat at their own risk.

Continue to the end of the alley then turn right back on to Soi Wanit 1. At this point you leave the narrow, congested streets behind. Keep walking for 400m (1,312ft) past the little old houses with wooden shutters and further on past the gem shops. When you reach the end of the road, continue almost straight over on to Songwat Rd. Wat Patuma Kongkha is on the right.

5 Wat Patuma Kongkha

A former execution site for royal criminals, Wat Patuma Kongkha has since gone through something of a metamorphosis. Inside the courtyard you will find rows of golden Buddhas and a haven of calm. Yet it was only in the mid-19th century, during the reign of Rama IV, known as King Mongkut, that the last royal victim, a cousin of

Renovated Buddha statues at Wat Patuma Kongkha, Bangkok

the king, was beaten to death with a club.

Leave Wat Patuma Kongkha and continue down Songwat Rd for 100m (328ft), then turn right down Soi Phanit Rang Si. This curves left into Soi Wanit 2 which after 700m (2,297ft) will bring you to Wat Kalawa, known as the Holy Rosary Church.

6 Wat Kalawa (Holy Rosary Church)

Originally constructed by Portuguese Catholics who fled from Ayutthaya to Thonburi after the city fell in 1767, Wat Kalawa has since been totally rebuilt. It remains an incongruous sight. Inside is a wooden pulpit along with stained-glass windows depicting episodes from the Old and New Testaments. There are even daily services in Thai and Chinese.

Leave the Holy Rosary Church and continue down Soi Wanit 2 until you reach the Royal Orchid Sheraton Hotel. From there you can catch an express boat or a taxi home.

Grand Palace

The most dazzling of all Bangkok's monuments, the Grand Palace complex lies behind massive white battlements in the heart of the old city. Built by successive monarchs of the Chakri dynasty, each crowning the glories of the last, it contains palaces and temples whose architecture spans over 200 years. It also contains the most highly revered Buddha image carved from a single block of fine jade, the Phra Kaeo Morakot (Emerald Buddha).

Dazzling and glittering Wat Phra Kaeo

Indeed, until King Rama IX, the present king, moved his residence to Chitladda Palace, following the unexplained death of his elder brother, Ananda Mahidol, it also housed the early monarchs.

Even today, the Grand Palace remains the true centre of royalty, used for state banquets and for the presentation of ambassadorial credentials. All the most important celebrations are held here, and even the simplest occasion, such as the king's birthday, recalls all the pageantry of ancient Siam.

A succession of palaces

Several great monuments dominate the palace grounds, each with its own architectural style, reflecting both the times and the tastes of its founder.

One of the finest is the Chakri Maha Prasad, built during the reign of King Chulalongkorn (1868–1910). This was designed by a British architect, but in Italian Renaissance style, reflecting the king's love of European architecture. On this has been superimposed the Siamese-style *prasad* (tower). Inside are reception rooms, as well as the throne

room where the king still receives foreign ambassadors on a niello throne under a nine-tiered white umbrella.

To the right of Chakri Maha Prasad is the Dusit Maha Prasad, a classical Thai palace, built in 1789; alongside is an exquisite pavilion called the Arporn Phimok Prasad or 'Disrobing Pavilion', used by the king to remove his ceremonial headgear.

Another fine building, and the only one currently open to visitors, is the Audience Hall of Amarin, built during the reign of Rama I (1782–1809). Everything about it speaks of regal splendour. Formerly the royal Court of Justice, it is now used as the coronation room; or for royal ceremonies (at which the king once presided from a throne concealed by curtains).

Beyond the Audience Hall lies the inner compound, the mysterious quarters in which female members of the royal families, royal concubines and court women once resided. Until the beginning of the 20th century, men were absolutely forbidden to enter the area. Times have changed and these days, although still closed to the general public, it is used by students of the Phra Tamnak Suankularb School, who specialise in the ancient court arts.

The Emerald Buddha

The pièce de résistance, and the most precious of all images in Thailand, is housed in the northeast corner of the palace compound, within Wat Phra Kaeo. The Emerald Buddha was supposedly discovered centuries ago in northern Thailand, when a bolt of lightning struck an old *chedi* (pagoda), revealing the image. The Buddha was briefly housed in the northern cities of Chiang Rai, Lampang and Chiang Mai, before being taken to Luang Prabang and

Vientiane by the Laotians. Finally, it was recovered and installed in Bangkok, amid great pomp, by Rama I.

Do not, however, expect some vast statue. The Buddha is just 0.75m (2^{1}/2ft) tall and is positioned high up on a gilded altar beneath an umbrella of gold. Invested in this

The fabled spires of the Grand Palace

fragile figure is a supernatural power beyond all others: it is believed that so long as the Emerald Buddha remains in Thai hands, the kingdom will be free. It is hardly surprising, then, that the image is surrounded in splendour. On the walls are paintings from the great *Ramakien* epic, while outside there are gold-embellished engravings and statues of mythological *kinarees* – half-bird, half-woman – said to inhabit the legendary Himalayan forests.

Photography is not allowed within Wat Phra Kaeo, but outside there is always a queue of people trying, surreptitiously, to aim their lenses between the gold panelled doors. *Five minutes' walk from the Tha Chang express boat pier on the Chao Phraya River and within easy reach of Wat Pho, Wat Arun, Wat Mahathat, Lakmuang and the National Museum. Wear reasonably formal clothes (no shorts or sleeveless tops). Open: daily 8.30am–3.30pm. Admission charge. Beware of touts.*

Jim Thompson's House

One of the most famous residents of Bangkok in the mid-20th century was the legendary Jim Thompson, a silk merchant, spy and connoisseur of fine antiques. He disappeared under mysterious circumstances in Malaysia's Cameron Highlands in 1967, but left behind, in Bangkok, a beautiful old teakwood house.

The house is full of works of oriental art, pots and statues dating as far back as the Lop Buri period (11th–14th century). It overlooks a silk weaving 'village' in the heart of the city, where skeins of brightly coloured silk are hung out to dry. With its small and lovely, luxuriant garden, it provides a wonderful feel of old Bangkok.

Guided tours are offered in several languages. Afterwards, you may be guided to Jim Thompson's shop on Surawong Road to buy the silk for which he became known. Beware of imitations, and of other shops that claim to be supplied by Thompson's.
Soi Kasem San 2, opposite the National Stadium on Rama I Rd. Open: daily 9am–5pm. Admission charge.

MARKETS

The biggest and best-known market in Bangkok is the Weekend Market at Chatuchak Park off Phahon Yothin Road (the last station on the BTS skytrain system), active from 6am to dusk on Saturdays and Sundays. This is the place to pick up old books as well as plants, acne cures and parrots, in addition to anything else that you could possibly dream of. For clothes, try Pratunam Market at the intersection of Ratchaprarop and Phetchaburi roads. For flowers and vegetables, try the Pak Khlong market at the foot of Memorial Bridge. For antiques, the Thieves Market off Yaowarat Road in China Town is still the favourite. Alternatively, just wander off any of the main streets. At some stage you are bound to come upon a small neighbourhood market.

Kamthieng House

Kamthieng House is another of the city's great old teakwood residences, dating back more than 130 years, and representing one of the finest examples of northern Thai architecture.

The house was originally brought down from the northern provinces to illustrate the typical old Thai Lanna-style construction with its sheds, barn and agricultural implements. Displays consist of old costumes and carvings along with the *ham yong* or 'sacred testicles' (carved lintels) said to preserve the fertility of its inhabitants.

141 Soi Asoke (Soi 21), Sukhumvit Rd. Open: Tue–Sat 9am–5pm. Admission charge.

Lakmuang Shrine

When Rama I founded Bangkok, he placed the trunk of a laburnum tree in the ground to commemorate the event and to appease the resident spirits. Lakmuang (which literally means 'City Pillar') has since been enlarged. It remains the place from which all distances in Thailand are measured, and it is hallowed above almost any other spot in Bangkok. Inside are several shrines where flowers, boiled eggs, joss sticks and, occasionally, bottles of whisky are offered.

At the southeast corner of the Pramane Grounds outside the Ministry of Defence on Sanam Luang.
Open: daily. Free admission.

Lumphini Park

Lumphini Park is a haven of calm in the centre of chaos. It lies within a stone's throw of the commercial centre, yet has a lake for boating, noodle stalls and shady walkways. Popular in the evening with joggers, and in the afternoon for picnics, the park is at its most crowded at dawn when people come to practise tai chi and drink snakes' blood from the stalls outside. For those with less athletic tastes, Soi Sarasin, the road that runs parallel to the northern exit, also has some of the best jazz bars in town.

On the corner of Silom Rd & Rama IV. Opposite the Dusit Thani Hotel.
Open: daily. Free admission.

The Jim Thompson House in Bangkok is a study in interior design and Thai furnishings

National Museum

A five-minute walk from the Grand Palace will bring you to one of the largest and finest museums in Southeast Asia. The National Museum houses a vast collection of exhibits and its English explanations offer the best starting point for anyone who wants to understand something of Thailand's cultural and artistic history.

Priceless exhibits are securely displayed

The exhibits cover more than 10,000 years, from the earliest traces of Neolithic man up to the present day, and they represent the best of the nation's works of art. Provincial museums in Chiang Mai, Sukhothai, Korat and Khon Kaen also have priceless exhibits, but they cannot compare in size or scope.

Indeed, the chief problem is that there is almost too much to absorb. Enthusiasts go back several times, and then again, for more. But even a small dip into the collection will be rewarded with invaluable insights into Thai culture, and provides an inkling of the power, ingenuity and artistry behind the monuments you see today.

A work of art

The starting point for any tour could well begin with the museum itself. The buildings were formerly part of an old palace belonging to the surrogate monarch (the king's deputy – a post later abolished), and date from 1782. Finest among them is the Buddhaisawan Chapel, with murals depicting scenes from the life of Buddha. Visitors should also see the Tamnak Daeng or 'Red House', a splendid structure dating from

the reign of Rama I (1782–1809). The next stop should be the fantastic skulls, the bronzes, and the pottery excavated from Ban Kao and Ban Chiang, evidence of a civilisation which may have thrived as far back as 10,000 years ago. These are to be found near the entrance, in the prehistory section, along with details about early trading routes and kingdoms.

The rest of the museum is divided into the original buildings and the two new wings, with a total of 42 different halls, each reflecting a different theme or period of history.

In the new south wing you will see the stone and bronze images of the Khmers who occupied vast areas of the kingdom from the 8th to the 11th century. Rooms 7 and 8 of the north wing are devoted to the Sukhothai period and contain some of the most beautiful Buddha images ever sculpted.

Other items not to miss include the funeral chariots in Room 17 (the largest of which is 12m (39ft) high, weighs 20.3 tonnes (20 tons), and took 290 people to move), and the warrior mounted on a life-sized elephant in Room 10. Outside that room there are shadow masks, a miniature train that King Mongkut

(Rama IV) presented to Queen Victoria, old photographs, textiles, puppets and flags, as well as royal games and musical instruments.

Organised tour

If you get the chance, take an organised tour. This is by far the best and most informative way of exploring the museum.

If you only have a couple of hours to spare, it is essential to decide on your priorities. Those with more time (or who make repeat visits) will, naturally, gain much more.

Outside the museum is a snackbar serving reasonably priced Western and Thai food. Adjacent to the National Museum is the National Theatre where drama and performances of Thai classical dance are presented. Occasionally, if you are lucky, you may

find that a display is scheduled. For details, check with the **Tourist Authority of Thailand**:

No. 4 Ratchadamnoen Nok Ave. On Na Phra That Rd, opposite the northwest corner of Sanam Luang, within easy walking distance of the Grand Palace, Lakmuang and Wat Mahathat. Tel: 0 2282 9773; www.tat.or.th Open: Wed–Sun 9am–4pm. Closed on public holidays. Tours: in English on Wed & Thu; French on Wed & Thu; German on Thu; and Japanese, second Wed of each month. Admission charge.

The museum contains artefacts from the Neolithic Age to the present Chakri dynasty

Tourists being shown a hooded cobra at the Snake Farm

Royal Barge National Museum

The magnificently adorned Royal Barges were once used for annual processions down the river. The King's barge, Suphanahong ('the Auspicious Swan'), is one of the most important. It is about 44m (144ft) long and requires 54 oarsmen. It is also the oldest and most ornately carved, with a great bauble dangling from the swan's beak at the front. The barges are now too frail for regular use, though they still make a colourful spectacle on very special occasions, such as a royal birth.

Off Khlong Bangkok Noi on the Thonburi side of the Chao Phraya River. The best way there is by long-tailed boat from Tha Chang pier near the Grand Palace. Open: daily 9am–5pm. Admission charge.

Siam Square

With its cinemas, its fashionable boutiques and its shopping centres, Siam Square tops anywhere else in the city as the heart of the young, the new and the trendy. This is the place to shop for up-market clothes, handicrafts and silks, but McDonald's hamburgers, Pizza Huts and videos are also present in

The Royal Barge National Museum, Bangkok

abundance. The square is especially busy at dusk and at weekends.

Silom Road

The heart of Bangkok's business district, known as Silom, is the place to find the big banks, airline offices, and shopping centres. A part of Silom is also known as Bangrak, meaning district of love. It is possibly no coincidence that here lies Patpong, the best-known red-light district in the world (*see p44*). Even if it is not your scene, everyone has to visit it. You will not have seen Bangkok otherwise.

Snake Farm

Snakes can be seen at the Thonburi Snake Farm or the Dusit Zoo, but the best of them are at the Queen Saowaba Institute. Visitors can watch the snakes being milked for serum on weekdays at 11am and 2.30pm, or at 11am on public holidays and weekends. The snakes include massive cobras, vipers and even the deadly krait. They are not, however, just there for tourists. They also serve the vital purpose of supplying serum to medical centres around the kingdom. *On the corner of Henri Dunant Rd and Rama IV Rd. Open: Mon–Fri 8.30am– 4.30pm, Sat–Sun 8.30am–noon. Admission charge.*

Suan Pakkard Palace

This collection of beautifully preserved wooden buildings is incongruously surrounded by cranes and new towerblocks. It was originally the home of the late Princess Chumphot of Nakhon Sawan in 1959, an enthusiastic gardener as well as a collector of antiques.

The luxuriant grounds of the palace contain numerous rare plants from all over the world, and collections of ancient Thai objets d'art, as well as the famous Lacquer Pavilion, which was put together from portions of two decayed buildings. *Near the Phayathai intersection on Si Ayutthaya Rd. Open: daily 9am–4pm. Admission charge.*

Sukhumvit Road

Sukhumvit Road lies to the east of the Silom business district and covers a rambling shopping, entertainment and residential area. Fashionable residences, international hotels, a great variety of restaurants and nightclubs are to be found in abundance, along with alternative nightspots, such as the Soi Cowboy hostess bars (*between Soi 21 and Soi 23*) and the similar Nana Plaza complex (*Soi 4*).

At one end, Sukhumvit Road extends into Phloen Chit Road, while to the east it becomes a busy highway that runs eventually to the Cambodian border. All roads off Sukhumvit are numbered in *sois* (alleys), with the even numbers running to the south and the odd numbers to the north.

A richly ornate lacquer pavilion in the grounds of Suan Pakkard

Bangkok at night

Patpong is the best-known nightspot in the city. Countless bars, restaurants and market stalls are found in this area. The bars mentioned here are some of the better-known ones. However, these sorts of bar are always on the move and, although they are likely to remain in the same area, an exact location has not been given.

Dressed up to the nines!

Catch a metered taxi or tuk tuk to the intersection of Silom Rd and Patpong 1 Rd, from where you can explore one of the world's best-known red-light districts.

Blue Sky Thai Boxing Bar

Thai boxing may be alien to Patpong, but then anything goes here. Get there before 10pm, when the show generally begins, and get a seat by the ring. *Muay-Thai* here may not be as skilful as in Bangkok's better known Lumphini and Ratchadamnoen stadiums, but for those with limited time it provides an idea of the skills involved. Between boxing bouts there are generally other forms of entertainment on offer. When you have seen enough boxing, explore the shopping stores that line the street.

King's Castle

Although *Newsweek* voted this the best bar in town several years ago, King's Castle is better known as the spot where Carol Thatcher, the daughter of the former British prime minister, was allegedly involved in a 'balloon show'. That was back in 1984 and the balloon show has since moved to other upstairs bars. Meanwhile, King's Castle continues to thrive.

Markets

Patpong is especially famous for its fake designer watches, T-shirts, CDs, VCRs and cassettes. Understandably, it is pointless to expect the same quality as the originals. Remember to bargain, and smile as much as you can (you generally get better bargains that way).

Once you have had your surfeit of markets, you could round the evening off at the Queen's Castle (*see opposite*).

Mizu's

History places the beginning of Patpong at the door of Mizu's. It was set up in 1954 and has continued selling Western food and Japanese specialities ever since. Do not expect girls, though. Mizu's is strictly for eating and taking in the past in a cosy atmosphere. Try a steak or one of the Japanese house specialities.

Patpong Road

Patpong is made up of three streets owned by an old Chinese rice-milling family called Patpong. Family patriarch Pong Pat bought the land as rice fields in the 1940s when Silom, the major road artery, was still a canal. Today the area has become the largest, most successful, and most popular nightlife destination in Thailand – and the Patpong family one of the richest in Thailand. To get a sense of the place, wander down Patpong Rd, but beware of touts who take you to second-floor 'clip joints' and try to charge you the earth. Always check prices for drink and entertainment first, and if in doubt, do not go in.

Peppermint

This is one of the oldest bars in the district, but with the modern decor that has become a hallmark of the changing times. When the first strip bar opened in 1969, the police tried to ban it. These days 'go-go dancing' is the rule in Patpong rather than the exception. Try a Mekong whisky and Coke. As with every other bar in Patpong, it is advisable to check the price first.

Queen's Castle

Queen's Castle is renowned for its live shows and for all the things people generally expect to find in Patpong. Normally it is packed with foreigners, and is reasonably priced, but, as with every bar, check prices on entry. In the old days, many of the first-floor rooms in Patpong were taken up by journalists' offices. These days, few of them would be able to afford the high rent.

The night market at Patpong, Bangkok

Temples

Bangkok's six most renowned temples are scattered around the city. They can be seen as part of a tour or combined with other sights around the capital.

Wat Arun (Temple of Dawn)

Bangkok's best-known landmark and once its tallest building, Wat Arun is undoubtedly the most spectacular of the riverside temples.

Constructed during the 19th century and subsequently enlarged during the reigns of Rama II and III, its *prang* (spire) measures 79m (259ft), and is covered almost entirely with fragments of multicoloured porcelain. For good views of the river climb the steps, but be careful because they are very steep and slippery. *Directly opposite Tha Tien pier on the Thonburi side of the Chao Phraya River. It is reached by baht boat. Open: daily 8.30am–5.30pm. Admission charge.*

Wat Benchamabophit (Marble Temple)

One of the most recent of Bangkok's temples, Wat Benchamabophit was only started in 1901 during the reign of King Chulalongkorn. It is built of milky white Carara marble, shipped at great expense from Italy, which makes this *wat* one of the most beautiful and popular in the city.

Inside the courtyard are over 50 statues of Buddha, and in the *bot* (main hall) are the ashes of King Chulalongkorn himself. The best time to visit is at dawn when the monks huddle under the trees on their early-morning alms round. *A short distance from the Dusit Zoo on Si Ayutthaya Rd. Open: daily 8am–5.30pm. Admission charge.*

Wat Mahathat

Known as the Temple of the Great Relic, Wat Mahathat was built before Bangkok was founded and is renowned, above all, as a centre for Buddhist philosophy and meditation. Visit it on Sundays and Buddhist holidays when an open-air market is held outside the temple premises.

WHAT IS WAT?

Thai temples have their own descriptive terms for their various distinctive features. Some of these are given here:

A *chedi* or stupa is a bell-like tower or pagoda in which relics of the Buddha, or some other important person, are kept.

A *prang* is a tall, finger-like spire that has a rounded top.

A *chofa* is a graceful finial extending from the roof.

A *prasad* is a tower sanctuary of Khmer origin.

A *bot* is an ordination hall, and a *viharn* is a hall for daily services.

Meditation classes are held in English on the second Saturday of the month, from 2–6pm.
On the Na Pra That Rd between the National Museum and Wat Phra Kaeo. Open: daily 7am–8pm. Free admission.

Wat Pho (Wat Chetupon)
The largest and one of the oldest of Bangkok's temples, Wat Pho was founded by King Rama I in the 16th century and contains some of the capital's finest architecture.

The highlight of a visit is the gigantic Reclining Buddha that lies at the northern end of the enclosure. The figure measures more than 46m (151ft) in length and 15m (49ft) in height. The soles of the feet have been inlaid with mother-of-pearl depicting the 108 auspicious signs of the Buddha.
At the southern corner of the Grand Palace on Maharat Rd. Open: daily 8am–6pm. Admission charge.

A solid gold Buddha at Wat Traimit, Bangkok

Wall detail at Wat Arun

Wat Saket
Perched on top of an artificial hill and reached by a flight of 318 steps, Wat Saket is popularly known as the Temple of the Golden Mount. At the top is a gilded *chedi* (pagoda), enshrining sacred relics of the Buddha. The temple was started during the reign of Rama III, but was not completed until the reign of Rama V. It offers some spectacular views of the city.
North of China Town on Baan Baat Rd. Open: daily 7.30am–5.30pm. Admission charge.

Wat Traimit
Wat Traimit's claim to fame is a 5.6-tonne (5.5-ton) Buddha, reputedly 700 or 800 years old, made of gold which was discovered in the 1950s when the East Asiatic Company took over the building. The image was originally encased in stucco, but while it was being moved by crane, it fell and the plaster casing broke, revealing the massive solid gold image beneath.
On the intersection of Yaowarat Rd and Charoen Krung Rd, near Hualamphong railway station. Open: daily 8am–5pm. Free admission.

Walk: Bangkok's temples

This walking tour takes in some of the most famous and most beautiful of Bangkok's 400 temples, as well as providing glimpses of markets, waterways and famous landmarks.

Allow 3 hours.

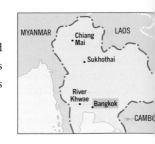

Take a metered taxi or tuk tuk to the Oriental Hotel off Charoen Krung Rd on the banks of the Chao Phraya River.

1 Oriental Hotel

Built in the late 19th century, the Oriental has become one of the best-known hotels in Asia. Joseph Conrad and Graham Greene both visited here, as did William Somerset Maugham, who nearly died of malaria here. If you are dressed with sufficient propriety (no flip-flops or vest tops), wander into the authors' lounge where you can see some of the old-worldly magic still at work. *Leave the hotel and turn right to the Oriental pier. Catch one of the Chao Phraya express boats plying upriver (to the right) and ask for Tha Rachini, the landing for Pak Khlong Market.*

2 Pak Khlong market

Bangkok's biggest wholesale market is a sensory delight of orchids, cabbages, wriggling frogs and chillies freshly brought in from the provinces by boat. Explore the little alleyways with their old wooden houses and treat yourself to exotic fruit sold at the sidestalls. *Wander back to Tha Rachini pier and catch the express boat to Tha Thien pier just a few minutes further upriver. Get off and take the tiny baht boat to the temple of Wat Arun, which lies directly opposite.*

3 Wat Arun

Formerly used as the royal temple by King Taksin of Thonburi, Wat Arun lost some of its royal notoriety after the deposed monarch was bludgeoned to death with a sandalwood club. But the temple, with its 104m (341ft) spire, remains one of Bangkok's best-known landmarks, and is covered in porcelain donated by loyal Chinese residents. Wander among the old monks' quarters at the back, with their wooden dwellings and the feel of rural Thailand. Note the beautiful lacquerware designs on the door of the temple. Look out for the famous snake!

Son et Lumière show: daily at 7pm, 8pm, 9pm & 9.15pm.

Cross back over the river to Tha Thien pier. Exit through the gate, and turn right along the outer walls of Wat Pho. The entrance is on your left.

4 Wat Pho

Famed for its vast reclining Buddha which is 45m long and has feet inlaid with mother-of-pearl, Wat Pho also contains more than 100 *chedis* (spire-like pagodas), a herbal clinic and a school of traditional massage. The *wat* was originally built in the 16th century and has since been restored to its original glory. On the way out, have your fortune read by an astrologer.

Leave Wat Pho, turn right, and walk 800m (2,625ft) along the massive white walls of the Grand Palace until you reach the entrance.

5 Grand Palace

Built by King Rama I, and extended and ennobled by his successors, the Grand Palace is one of the most important sights in Bangkok. It has enough to occupy the visitor for at least a day (*see pp36–8*). A brief tour can be made into the main buildings and the famous Wat Phra Kaeo, the Temple of the Emerald Buddha.

On the way out, pass the ticket counter and turn right immediately for the Royal Thai Decorations and Coin Pavilion.

6 Royal Thai Decorations and Coin Pavilion

Inside the pavilion is a magnificent collection of ceramic coins and silver money used from the early 11th century. Wander upstairs to see a selection of royal crowns, jewelled swords, brocaded robes and carved betel-nut objects.

Leave the museum and the Grand Palace, turn right, and, almost directly opposite, you will see the vast open green known as Sanam Luang.

7 Sanam Luang

A former cremation ground for kings and the place where the weekend market used to be held, Sanam Luang is also the spot where the early Chakri monarchs used to exercise their white elephants. Today the grounds are popular with walkers, kite-flyers and those selling snacks of kebabs and fried grasshoppers.

From Sanam Luang, catch a taxi or tuk tuk *home or take an express boat from the Tha Chang pier opposite the Grand Palace.*

Kite-flying at Sanam Luang

In towns and cities all over Thailand, the first light of dawn brings lines of monks in their saffron robes on to the streets to begin their daily round for alms. Men and women who have risen early especially to prepare foods, will place rice and fruit or flowers in the monk's bowl, *wai* (bowing) as they do so, and asking for a blessing. This centuries-old practice still has a large and faithful following throughout the kingdom.

Buddhism occupies a very special niche in Thai culture. It is more than just a religion – it can be a whole way of life or simply a way of hope. There are five rules of moral conduct that the Buddhist laypeople are expected to observe.

They are not 'commandments' but 'precepts', in the sense that Buddha never commanded people to follow them, but if followed they will bring happiness.

The five 'precepts' are: to abstain from taking the life of sentient beings; to abstain from taking possession of anything that has not been given by its owner; to abstain from sexual misconduct; to abstain from lying or evil speech; and to abstain from intoxicating drinks, which are the primary cause of negligence.

More than 90 per cent of the population practise Theravada Buddhism in some way, either by giving robes to the monks or by giving them food. Good deeds, Buddhists believe, will be returned in kind, and merits gained will bring more merit and the promise of a better life in the next world.

In the *wats* (temples), men as young as 20 join the order for anything from three weeks to a lifetime, meditating, and strictly following the 227 Buddhist precepts in the quest for selflessness.

Others, known as novices, serve their time looking after the monks and receiving education. Monk ordination ceremonies are commonplace, with 'mass ordinations' taking place at several of the most famous temples on special religious days.

Village life evolves around the temple. It is the heart of social life, with many temple fairs being held during the year, involving the selling of local products, shadow puppet shows and games.

The temple is also an option for people with nowhere to stay. The monks always welcome the homeless.

Images of Buddhism: people at prayer offer flowers and burn joss sticks at shrines and temples; monks are distinguished by their dress

Waterways

'The highways of Bangkok are not streets or roads, but rivers and canals' wrote Sir John Bowring in 1855. That may have been the case in the 19th century, but these days it is something of a simplification. Most of Bangkok's old *khlongs* (canals) are now tarmac-covered highways, but a number of them have survived, and travelling around them is still one of the great joys that the 'City of Angels' has to offer.

Thonburi's floating market

The main waterway is the Chao Phraya River which cuts through the city and carries rice barges down from the central plains. Off this main artery run the *khlongs*, small waterways where life has changed little over the past decades.

Here you may see children swimming, and older people draped in sarongs, washing themselves. But if you are tempted to join them in the water, think again. The Chao Phraya River is now so polluted that you might need a two-week holiday just to recover.

On the khlongs

The easiest way to get around the *khlongs* is to catch one of the Chao Phraya express taxi boats that speed up and down the river, stopping at the Oriental, the Sheraton and many other popular landmarks. These boats will take you all the way up to Nontha Buri and are very cheap.

Alternatively, hire a long-tailed boat (*reua hang yao*) which will take you to the Thonburi floating market and the rural dwellings around Khlong Ban Dan and Khlong Bangkok Yai. Prices are higher and you pay by the hour. Hotels also organise river trips to Ayutthaya, as well as dinner cruises; advance booking is essential.

Perhaps the most enjoyable way of exploring the waterways (and best value for money) is to take one of the public long-tailed boats which, for a handful of *baht*, will take you to the smaller *khlongs* where foreigners are the exception rather than the rule.

Public boats

The following public boats run regularly throughout the day and provide delightful glimpses of river life, although they may be crowded.

Chao Phraya River Express: departs from Wat Rajsingkron wharf every 15 minutes between 5.30am and 6pm stopping at 35 piers, including Tha Chang (Grand Palace) and Tha Thien (Wat Pho).

Khlong Mon: departs every 30 minutes from Tha Thien Pier behind Wat Pho between 6.30am and 6pm. Sights include riverside temples and orchid farms.

Khlong Bang Koo Wiang and Khlong Bang Yai: departs from Tha Chang pier near the Grand Palace every 30 minutes, between 6.30am and 11pm. This trip passes the Royal Barge National Museum.
Khlong Om: departs from Nontha Buri's Phibul Songkram pier every 15 minutes between 4am and 8pm. Attractions include durian plantations, temples and Thai-style houses.
Cross-river Ferries: for short trips across the Chao Phraya River, boats operate from Tha Thien pier to Wat Arun and from Tha Saphan Phut pier to Pracha Thipok Road. Timings are subject to change without notice.

Thonburi floating market

The pride of Bangkok's tourist industry became commercialised so many years ago that it has almost ceased to exist as a genuine market. Even so, the area

around, known as Khlong Bangkok Yai and Khlong Bangkok Noi (literally 'Big' and 'Little' canal), remains an endless source of fascination with its coconut palms, old warehouses and new concrete Tudor-style residences studded haphazardly along the river bank. The floating market can be reached either by hiring a private long-tailed boat from along the river, or by joining one of the group tours that leave at regular intervals from the Tha Chang pier outside the Grand Palace. The boats will take you to a snake farm and to the glorious Royal Barge National Museum. They will also stop briefly at Wat Arun.

You will not be the only one doing the trip, but if you do not have the time to visit the more genuine market at Damnoen Saduak *(see p61)* this is a wonderful way to get a glimpse of the old Bangkok, the Venice of the East.

Travelling by river in a *khlong* is the easiest way to get about in busy Bangkok

Tour: Old Thonburi District

This is one of the least visited areas of town, with glimpses of the old Bangkok and the chance to wander a little more adventurously away from the crowds.
Allow 3 hours.

Begin at the Tha Saphan Phut express boat landing at the foot of Memorial Bridge and catch the baht ferry that crosses the Chao Phraya River to Pracha Thipok Rd on the opposite bank.

1 Memorial Bridge (Phra Buddha Yotfa Bridge)

King Rama VII opened this first bridge across the Chao Phraya River on 6 April 1932. Two months later a revolution forced the king to give up absolute rule in Thailand. Memorial Bridge is one of more than ten in the city crossing the Chao Phraya and connecting Bangkok to Thailand's former capital, Thonburi.
Disembark on the far side of the river. Follow Pracha Thipok Rd for about 100m (328ft) until you see Wat Prayoonwong on the corner of Thetsaban 1 Rd.

2 Wat Prayoonwong

The 'Turtle Temple', Wat Prayoonwong, contains vast numbers of these reptiles that are fed with papaya and sliced bananas by people who wish to win merit and secure themselves a better life in the next earthly cycle. The temple was built in the reign of King Rama III by a member of Thailand's powerful Bunnag family and is especially noted for its fine doors decorated with mother-of-pearl.

Leave the temple and walk down Thetsaban 1 for about 200m (656ft) until you glimpse a church tower on your right. To get to Santa Cruz Church you must cross through the graveyard, which also doubles up as a car park.

3 Santa Cruz Church

One of the most delightful of the old buildings on the river bank, Santa Cruz Church stands on the site of an earlier and even more magnificent edifice. The original church was built more than 200 years ago by a collection of Portuguese adventurers, traders and missionaries, but was torn down in 1913 to make way for the new. Note the graveyard where the former residents have been interred in concrete vaults, each of the deceased identified by a photograph. Visitors will find this old Portuguese section of the city around the church a quiet oasis, far from the hustle and bustle of modern-day Bangkok.
Leave the church and continue west along the narrow walkways that run parallel to the river. You will soon enter the district known as the Old Farang quarter.

4 Old Farang quarter

At the start of the 20th century, the area around Santa Cruz Church was still popular with Westerners, known as *farangs* in Thai, who resided in spacious villas within easy boating distance of China Town and the Grand Palace. Though the *farangs* and most of the villas are gone, you can still see some charming old wooden houses, closely packed in a network of interconnecting *sois* (alleys). Nobody seems to hurry here; it is as if the world has left this piece of Bangkok behind.

Aiming to keep parallel to the river, follow one of the narrow walkways that snakes its way through the wooden houses. After less than 150m (492ft) you will emerge at the main road (Soi Wat Kalayanamit), where you must turn right to the temple of the same name. If you lose your way just ask any of the locals for Wat Kalayanimit.

5 Wat Kalayanimit

The majestic old riverside temple of Wat Kalayanimit actually predates Bangkok, although it was subsequently renovated in the 19th century, during the reign of Rama III, to house an enormous seated statue called Luang Paw Toh or Big

Buddha. The Chinese also worship the statue and hold a grand homage-paying fair annually in its honour. Inside are fine murals and several Chinese shrines. Outside, in the spacious compound, the large bronze bell is reputed to be the biggest in Thailand.

Walk to the river bank, about 100m (328ft) away, from where you will see some house barges.

6 House barges

Once to be found all along the waters of the Chao Phraya River, old rice barges are now the exception rather than the rule. The few that remain still ply the 'Mother of Rivers', carrying sand, charcoal and rice all the way down from Nakhon Sawan in the Central Plains.

From the house barges, walk east (downriver) along a narrow path that runs to the Tha Reva Kalaya landing. Catch the regular baht boat that crosses back over the Chao Phraya River to Tha Rachini pier and the Pak Khlong market. From here you can take a taxi or tuk tuk home.

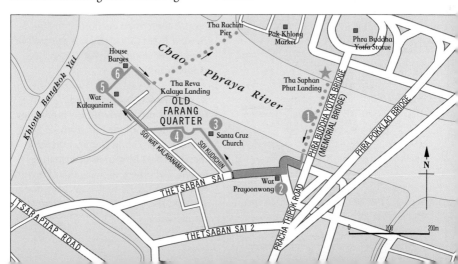

Tour: Bangkok's Chao Phraya River

This delightful river trip provides views of city life and of some fine monuments.
Allow 3 hours.

Start at Wat Rajsingkorn pier on Charoen Krung Rd, near the Menam Hotel. Catch a Chao Phraya express boat heading upstream (to the right) and ask for Krung Thon Bridge. After passing Taksin Bridge you will see the Old Customs House on your right, just past the Oriental Hotel.

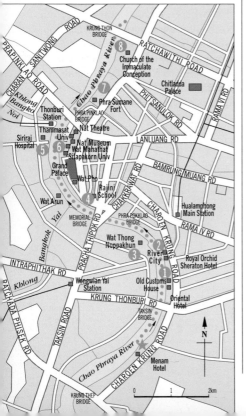

1 Old Customs House

Built in the late 19th century, this delightful old building hugging the river bank was once the main customs house for Bangkok. It is now used by the city's fire brigade. The building does, however, give an idea of what the whole riverfront may once have looked like.
From the Old Customs House, the boat passes the Royal Orchid Sheraton Hotel. Next door is River City.

2 River City

The first of several modern shopping centres on the river, and a three-storey haven for antique explorers, River City bustles with silk shops, ancient elephant statues from Laos and rare pieces from Cambodia. On the first Sunday of every month there is an auction.
Beyond River City on the left you will glimpse the outline of Wat Thong Noppakhun.

3 Wat Thong Noppakhun

Buddhists can clearly see the humorous side of life. Until the mid-19th century Wat Thong Noppakhun was distinguished by murals of urinating angels and others showing their bare buttocks. King Rama IV was horrified and had the controversial paintings retouched.

Further upriver from Wat Thong Noppakhun, you will see the Rajini School on the right bank after Memorial Bridge.

4 Rajini School

A Neo-Classical building houses the Rajini School which was founded in 1904 by Queen Saowapa Pongsri to educate young women. Although something of a revolutionary concept at the time (until then, only boys were considered worthy of education), the school went on to become one of Thailand's most pre-eminent academic establishments.
From the Rajini School, the boat passes the Wat Arun (on the left) and the Grand Palace (on the right). Further down on the left bank is the modern white façade of the Siriraj Hospital.

5 Siriraj Hospital

It may look ordinary from the outside, but the Siriraj Hospital museum contains some unusual specimens, including foetuses, the skulls of electrocuted criminals, and the body of the most notorious criminal of the lot: Si Oui, the Chinese mass-murderer who strangled seven children and, for his sins, is now preserved in formaldehyde.
Beyond Siriraj Hospital, on the right bank, is Thammasat University.

6 Thammasat University

Founded just before World War II, Thammasat is a radical educational institution. During student uprisings in 1973 and 1976 protesting against military influence, army leaders sent in tanks and helicopters, and many people were killed or injured. This paved the way for a new constitution.

After passing Phra Pinklao Bridge, you will see the Phra Sumane Fort on your right.

7 Phra Sumane Fort

The octagonal fort which looms over the river was originally built in the late 18th century, during the reign of King Rama I, as a defence against invaders. The present structure, however, only dates from Bangkok's bicentenary (1982).
Shortly before you arrive at the next bridge (Krung Thon Bridge) you will see the Church of the Immaculate Conception on the right.

8 Church of the Immaculate Conception

Built around 1674 by Father Louis Laneau, the church served as the religious centre for Portuguese Catholics. It was rebuilt in 1837 and contains many beautiful statues of the Virgin.
After passing under the next bridge, either alight at Sang Hee pier and catch an express boat back, or continue to Nontha Buri, the bustling market town which lies 30 minutes further upriver. Be warned, however: the last boat back leaves Nontha Buri at 6pm.

The Queen Sirikit *chedi* atop Doi Inthanon, Thailand's highest point

BANGKOK ENVIRONS
Ayutthaya

Ayutthaya is not considered a high point in glorious Siam for nothing. The great city, once the nation's capital, survived 33 kings, numerous invasions and 400 years of turbulent history. In so doing, it established itself as one of the major civilisations of the 14th to the 18th centuries. Louis XIV of France sent his emissaries to the kingdom, while the British and Portuguese traders came to buy spices and enjoy the largesse of its god-like rulers.

Only after numerous wars did the Burmese, invading on the backs of elephants, finally quell Ayutthaya in 1767. When they did so, they left little doubt as to who the victors were. All but 10,000 of the inhabitants were massacred or taken into slavery, gold Buddhas were melted down, and the place was left in desolation.

Resplendent even in decay; the ruins of Wat Ratburana, Ayutthaya

Today, the ruins of this once great city attract tourists from all over the world with its weeds and dreams, and the feel of a bygone era.

76km (47 miles) north of Bangkok. Trains leave about 20 times a day from Hualamphong railway station, and buses leave every 40 minutes from the Northern Bus Terminal on Phahon Yothin Rd. If you are without your own transport, it is best to hire a bicycle rickshaw and ask for a short tour. The most popular way of getting there is by boat on the day trip run by the Oriental Hotel which leaves the hotel pier at 8am. Passengers return by coach around 6pm. For reservations, contact: Oriental Hotel, 48 Oriental Ave. Tel: 0 2659 9000; www.mandarinoriental.com

Bang Pa-In Summer Palace

A short ride from the ancient city of Ayutthaya is the fabled summer palace of Bang Pa-In, the country residence of a succession of monarchs that dates from the 17th century. The original palace was founded by King Prasat Thong.

The highlight of the palace is the exquisite 19th-century Aisawan Tippaya Asna pavilion. This sits in the centre of a lake, where King Chulalongkorn, a man known for his European tastes, would watch the world go by.

Nearby is the classic-style royal residence of Warophat Phiman, the Saphakhan Ratchaprayun, and the Ho Withun Thasana, endearingly known as the 'Sage's Lookout'.

20km (12¹/₂ miles) to the south of Ayutthaya. Bang Pa-In is included in most tours.

The Bang Pa-In Summer Palace with the pavilion in front

Minibuses also leave from the Chao Prom Market in Ayutthaya. Open: daily 8.30am–4.30pm. Admission charge.

Chao Sam Phraya Museum

This contains exquisite Ayutthaya-period stone and bronze Buddha images and a fine collection of carved door panels.
On Rotchana Rd. Open: Wed–Sun 9am–4pm. Admission charge.

Viharn Phra Mongkol Bophit

This contains one of Thailand's largest bronze images of the Buddha; it was sacked in 1767 but has since been restored in its original style.
Off Sri San Phet Rd. Open: daily 8.30am–5pm.

Wat Mahathat

This temple was built by King Ramesuan in 1384. When the government undertook to restore the ruins in 1956, the *wat* was found to contain a buried chest containing a relic of the Buddha inside a golden casket.
On Naresuan Rd. Open: daily 8.30am–4.30pm. Admission charge.

Wat Ratburana

Built in 1424 by King Borommaracha II, this *wat* commemorates his two sons who killed each other in an elephant duel.
Opposite Wat Mahathat. Open: daily 8.30am–4.30pm. Admission charge.

Wat Sri San Phet

The most important of Ayutthaya's temples, this housed a gold, standing Buddha until the Burmese melted it down. What remains are three *chedis* (pagodas) containing the ashes of King Borom Trai Lokanat and his two sons.
Off Sri San Phet Rd. Open: daily 8.30am–4.30pm. Admission charge.

Ancient City

Billed as the largest outdoor museum in Thailand, Ancient City is a must for everyone.

The city covers no less than 80 hectares (198 acres) and consists of scaled-down models of wats, palaces and ruins (as well as a few originals), laid out in an area the shape of Thailand. Even some buildings that no longer exist are on show, recreated from ancient records.

So heavily promoted is the Ancient City that many tourists go expecting to discover one of Thailand's ancient capitals. But if you are looking for an idea of Thailand's vast architectural riches, or a sense of the many centuries of years of its history, you will undoubtedly find this one of the best sights in the kingdom.

34km (21 miles) to the southeast of Bangkok. Advice and information, as well as a guidebook to the Ancient City, can be obtained from the Ancient City Co, Democracy Monument, Ratchadamnoen Ave. Alternatively, catch bus No. 8 or 11 from the Eastern Bus Terminal on Sukhumwit Rd to Samut Prakan. Open: daily 8am–5pm. Admission charge.

Crocodile Farm

Some 60,000 crocodiles are to be found at the kingdom's biggest farm, in Samut Prakan Province, 30km ($18^1/2$ miles) from Bangkok, performing shows when they are alive, and sold as handbags when dead. Hourly shows, some featuring crocodile wrestling, take place. At other times, you can watch them basking in the sun or semi-submerged in an ink-black lake.

Traditional Thai houses in the Ancient City

A keeper and his croc, Samut Prakan

When you have had enough of crocodiles, there are plenty of other animals on show, including elephants, snakes, birds and monkeys, as well as a host of food stalls, picnic spots and other sundry amusements for children. *25km (15¹/₂ miles) southeast of Bangkok near the town of Samut Prakan. Travel agents in Bangkok undertake half-day and full-day tours. Alternatively, catch bus No. 25 from the Eastern Bus Terminal on Sukhumwit Rd to Samut Prakan. Open: daily 7am–6pm. Admission charge.*

Damnoen Saduak

For a glimpse of the good old days when people traded from boats on canals, ignore the commercialised Thonburi floating market and take a tour to the small village of Damnoen Saduak.

From the break of dawn, the place is transformed into a watery market of diminutive paddlers. Traders, selling 10 different kinds of bananas, spiky durians, the king of all fruits, and tender grilled kebabs with chilli sauces, paddle around the canals, while others barter in a deluge of colour that could come straight from a fairy tale.

You can either watch the traders from along the walkways, where there is a land-based market selling handicrafts and coconuts, full of running dogs and smiling children, or you can take a boat tour from the Chang Pier near the Grand Palace and join the milling crowds on the water.

Most tours include a boat trip around the maze of canals, where fruits and vegetables are brought in from all over the central plains region. Some excursions include a trip to a nearby snake farm.

Although Damnoen Saduak has become a major tourist spot, with shops and boutiques catering to the coachloads of day trippers, the scenes of yesteryear are more than enough to make up for this. Most people leave with a camera full of good pictures and some of their finest memories of Thailand. *109km (68 miles) to the southwest of Bangkok, reached by bus from Bangkok's Southern Bus Terminal via Nakhon Pathom. It is best to take a day tour, choosing one that gets you to the market very early in the morning. Free admission.*

Boats at the floating market

Kanchana Buri

Mention the name Kanchana Buri and two visions come to mind: one of war, the other of peace and calm. For Kanchana Buri is both a beautiful province and the location of the Khwae (Kwai) Bridge, which was to become famous through Pierre Boulle's chilling novel and the subsequent film.

During World War II, hundreds of thousands of prisoners were put to work on the bridge and railway, which was designed to connect Japanese-controlled Singapore with Rangoon (Yangon), the Burmese capital. Many died of malaria, others from beatings, starvation and exhaustion.

Although part of the bridge was bombed in 1945, you can still see the original version (with its rebuilt central section). It spans the Khwae Yai River just 5km (3 miles) north of Kanchana Buri town, and carries the railway from Bangkok to the village of Nam Tok. Under the bridge, enterprising salesmen use their rafts as floating restaurants.

130km (81 miles) west of Bangkok. A train leaves at 7.45am daily from Thonburi railway station, taking two to three hours. Buses leave every 15 minutes from Bangkok's Southern Bus Terminal. For the more up-market accommodation on the river, make reservations through Bangkok travel agents prior to departure.

War Memorials

Victims of the war are remembered in two cemeteries and by a Japanese memorial. The Chung Kai War Cemetery lies on the banks of the Khwae Noi River, 20 minutes outside of town, and the Kanchana Buri War Cemetery is on Saeng Chuto Road near the town's railway station.
On Paak Phraek Rd, there is also the Jeath War Museum. Open: 8.30am–6pm. Admission charge.

National Parks

Most people come to Kanchana Buri these days to enjoy the quiet environs, to take river rafting trips on the Khwae, or

The bridge over the River Khwae

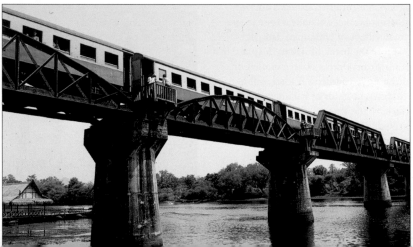

A traditional rope and log bridge complements the lush, unspoilt beauty of the forest

to explore the sapphire mines at Bo Ploi, 50km (31 miles) north.

More adventurous travellers or those with more time can use Kanchana Buri as a stepping stone to the town of **Sangkhla Buri**, 200km (124 miles) to the northwest, near the Myanmar border, or the two nearby national parks, **Erawan** (72km/44^1/$_2$ miles north) and **Sai Yok** (100km/62 miles west), which offer beautiful, unspoilt scenery and waterfalls.

There is no need to slum it, either. Luxury developments along the way allow visitors to explore during the day and relax at night. Some of the raft complexes have restaurants and swimming pools. The River Khwae Village (*tel: 0 3459 1055*) has a zoo.

Khao Yai National Park

Tigers and elephants may not be a common sight at Khao Yai, but they do exist, along with monkeys, black bears, Asian wild dogs, and some of the kingdom's most colourful birdlife. The nearest national park to Bangkok, Khao Yai ('Big Mountain') is also one of the

kingdom's largest, with more than 2,000sq km (772sq miles) of evergreen forest scattered with teak and mahogany. At weekends, the park gets extremely crowded and some of the wildlife, understandably, makes itself scarce. Warm clothes are recommended.

Visitors who are fortunate may come across great slaty woodpeckers, and the park also has one of the highest concentrations of hornbills in the country. A network of paths cuts through much of the park, and with the help of maps you can hike to the elephant watch tower and to the beautiful waterfalls of Heo Suwat and Heo Narok. Ideally, it is best to have a guide and transport. In the evening, elephant-spotting tours are arranged by the national park lodge using spotlights to 'freeze' the animals.

198km (123 miles) from Bangkok. Thai State Railways organise one-day tours which leave Bangkok's Hualamphong station at 6am and return the same evening, but you must book in advance. Khao Yai can also be reached by train and bus to Pak Chong, the nearest town, from where you must catch a songthaew *(truck taxi) to the park headquarters.*

The war cemetery at Kanchana Buri

Tour: From Bangkok to the River Khwae

This takes you by train to the historic bridge over the River Khwae (Kwai), for a short trip down the river, a visit to the war cemetery, and return to Bangkok.
Day trip.

Catch a taxi or express boat to Thonburi train station (also known as Bangkok Noi) on the western side of the Chao Phraya River, and buy a day return ticket to Kanchana Buri.

Breakfast at the Thonburi Market, next door to the railway station, then catch the train that departs at 7.35am sharp for Kanchana Buri and Nam Tok. The carriages are non air-conditioned third-class. No reservations are possible.

1 The Kanchana Buri Express
Leaving the old capital of Thonburi, the train cuts west into the area known as the central plains, going as far as Nam Tok, a small village marking the end of the line.

At Nakhon Pathom, which you reach after one hour, you will glimpse a vast pagoda on the left. This is one of the biggest in the world, and was built on the spot where Buddhism was first brought to Thailand in the 3rd century BC by missionaries sent out by Emperor Ashoka of India.

The train continues through rice paddies and tapioca plantations, stopping first at Kanchana Buri, then, three minutes later, at the Khwae Bridge Station where you should get out.

2 Khwae Bridge
This, the most famous and chilling bridge in modern history, was built in 1943 by Allied prisoners of war for the Japanese. The central spans of the bridge were blown up in 1945, and subsequently rebuilt with war reparation funds. The rest of the bridge is original, and it continues to be used by trains and

Map not to scale

pedestrians. Note the old steam engine at the outdoor museum, alongside the station, used during World War II. *Walk over the Khwae Bridge and explore the other side. Then walk down the river to the restaurant and boat landing stage.*

3 River Khwae

The tributaries Khwae Yai and Khwae Noi join at Kanchana Buri to form the Mae Klong River. For a pleasant hour's trip, hire a long-tailed boat from near the restaurant, and ask to be taken on the standard trip to the cave, the cemetery and the museum. *As you go downriver, the boat will take the right fork up the Khwae Noi until you reach Wat Thum Khao Phun on the right.*

4 Wat Thum Khao Phun

The main attraction of this *wat* is a small and poorly lit cave. Years ago, it was rumoured to contain gold left by the fleeing Japanese army at the end of World War II (as recently as March 2001, searches were organised by local officials, but nothing was found). Like many caves in Thailand, it has Buddha images placed in many of the recesses. *From Wat Thum Khao Phun, the boat will take you to the Chung Kai War Cemetery.*

5 Chung Kai War Cemetery

More than 16,000 prisoners of war lost their lives building the so-called 'Death Railway'. They are remembered in two beautifully maintained graveyards built by the Commonwealth War Graves Commission. Some of the 1,750 memorial stones in the Chung Kai Cemetery bear the 'Known Unto God'

inscription used for unknown soldiers. *Leaving the war cemetery, the boat will take you back to the junction of the two rivers and up the Mae Klong to the JEATH War Museum.*

6 JEATH War Museum

Established by the venerable Phra Thep Panyasuthee, in memory of the prisoners who lost their lives, the museum houses a collection of items related to the construction of the railway. The bamboo huts are replicas of those used by Allied prisoners of war. The paintings inside give some idea of their human suffering. Outside are weapons and an old field telephone. *Leaving the war museum, the boat will take you back to the Khwae Bridge railway station, from where the train departs for Bangkok in mid-afternoon, arriving back at Thonburi railway station at about 6pm. From the station, catch a taxi or boat home.*

Floating houses on the Khwae River near Kanchana Buri

In early November, the fields of central Thailand turn from green to golden brown: villagers descend into the paddies and the crop, known to the Thais as *khao suai* or 'beautiful rice', is harvested. Every year, Thailand grows over 25 million tonnes of rice, more than any other country in the world. More than half of the population participates in the harvest in some way.

Ploughing takes place with the aid of water buffalo or, in most communities, with tractors. Once the labour is finished, the fields are watered through a complex series of irrigation channels flowing from nearby rivers, streams and canals. The rice seedlings are planted by hand just before the rains begin.

In three months, the rice in the fields is ready for harvest. Once again, villagers go out in large groups, working with sickles. The cut rice is spread in the fields to dry for several days, then arranged in sheaves and taken to the family compound to be bought by wholesalers, for both the domestic market and export.

Despite the back-breaking manual toil, most workers in the fields receive meagre wages – but it keeps the

population relatively prosperous and, over the centuries, rice has probably been the biggest cause of stability in the kingdom. The importance of this crop for every Thai, rural or urban, can be seen every May when the Royal Ploughing Ceremony is held. With Brahmin rites, grains of rice are blessed and

scattered as lucky charms to farmers who come to Bangkok from all over the kingdom to try and catch some. A procession of public figures, dressed in white and gold and carrying a plough, passes before His Majesty the King of Thailand and his royal guard.

Various stages of the rice harvest, after which the stubble is burnt off and the paddy can be planted once again

In 1999, massive floods badly damaged the crop, and some of the poorest areas of Thailand suffered the most. Farmers staged a 'sit-in' outside Government House in Bangkok to protest against the government's lack of response.

In January 2001, the billionaire businessman, Thaksin Shinawatra, while campaigning for the post of Prime Minister, promised financial assistance to all local farming communities to help develop and modernise farming methods. The support of the farming community was vital to his subsequent electoral victory.

Lop Buri

The old town of Lop Buri, some 154km (95¹/₂ miles) north of Bangkok, is an amalgam of almost every chapter in Thailand's history. During the Dvaravati period (6th to 10th centuries), it was inhabited by Lawa people who called the town Lavo. In 950, it fell to the Khmers, who ruled it until the 13th century. In the 13th century, the shrewd kings of Ayutthaya established a second capital here in case their city fell to the warring Burmese. These days, modern shopping arcades complete the spectrum of architectural styles.

Trains leave from Hualamphong station 11 times a day, taking 2½ hours. Buses leave regularly from the Northern Bus Terminal on Kampaengphet 2 Rd.

Phra Narai Rajanivet

The highlight of Lop Buri for most visitors is this royal palace, former home to King Narai of Ayutthaya, one of the town's most intriguing characters. It was he who, in the 17th century, won the heart of Louis XIV's French emissaries and who even made Constantine Phaulkon, a Greek, his prime minister. Narai was finally usurped, but the huge battlemented walls, the ruins of the king's elephant stables, and a small museum can still be seen.

Sorasak Rd. Open: daily 8am–6pm. Admission charge.

Phraprang Sam Yod

Framed against the main-line railway to Bangkok are the old Khmer ruins of Phraprang Sam Yod. The temple, named after its three impressive *prangs* (spires), is typical of the Lop Buri style, and was built in the 13th century. Monkeys scamper around the nearby shrine of San Phra Karn.

On Wichayen Rd, near the railway track. Open: daily 8am–6pm. Admission charge.

The majestic Khmer ruins at Sam Yod

Every tourist's aim in Thailand

Houseboats and markets

Other temples worth visiting are Wat Phra Sri Mahathat, a lofty, 12th-century Khmer temple situated opposite the railway station, and the Brahminic shrine of San Phra Kahn, next to the level crossing. Two other sights not to be missed are the wooden houseboats on the river and the nearby busy market selling fruits, flowers and beautiful woven baskets.

Nakhon Pathom

There is only one reason to come to Nakhon Pathom, and that is to see the *chedi* (pagoda), said to be the tallest in the world. The *chedi*, which resembles an upturned ice-cream cornet, is over 120m (394ft) high and is supposed to mark the place where Buddhism was first brought by Indian missionaries in the 3rd century BC.

The huge, honey-coloured *chedi* was begun in 1853, during the reign of King Mongkut, when the much older *chedi*

that lies within the big one underwent considerable renovation. Later, the outer *chedi* was encased in gold-coloured tiles from China.

Nakhon Pathom is famous for its fruits; you may come across the famous *som-o* (pomelo), the luscious fruit that has become a staple of the provincial economy. It is harvested in August and November and sold throughout the country.

59km (36¹/₂ miles) west of Bangkok. Trains leave from Hualamphong railway station 10 times a day, taking 1½ hours. Buses leave every 20 minutes from the Southern Bus Terminal on Boromratchchannani Rd, from 6am–10.30pm. Day tours from Bangkok are generally combined with a trip to the floating market at Damnoen Saduak (see p61).

Rose Garden

Set in beautiful, lush surroundings on the banks of Thachin River, the Rose Garden is designed for those who want a touch of calm and colour away from the city. Cultural shows begin daily at 2.45pm with a programme that includes Thai folk dancing, Thai boxing, cock-fighting, and sword duels. There is also a swimming pool and the opportunity to go boating or waterskiing. Some visitors find the place too commercialised, even by Thai standards, but the beauty of the garden is remarkable. Nearby are a golf course and hotel.

32km (20 miles) west of Bangkok. Trips can be arranged by contacting the Rose Garden office in Bangkok. Tel: 0 3432 2588, www.rose-garden.com. Open: daily 8am–6pm. Admission charge.

Northern Thailand

CHIANG MAI

Almost everyone visits Chiang Mai at some stage of their visit to Thailand, for the northern capital and the kingdom's second largest city appears to have everything that Bangkok does not: a life that is slower, a population that is more manageable, and the feel of a fast-developing province rather than of a major city.

That is not to say that Chiang Mai is provincial. Commercially, it is now a thriving centre producing countless items for export worldwide. But the town has the unique advantage of a mountain setting, a cooler, temperate climate, and, during the months of spring, some of the most beautiful flowers that you will ever come across. Furthermore, it is a major staging post for trekking in the hill district and for visiting hill tribes, migrants from Myanmar and Laos, whose dress and handicrafts lure so many visitors from the West.

Chiang Mai itself is also the handicrafts centre of Thailand and the producer of fine lacquerware ceramics, hill-tribe clothes, jewellery and even opium pipes.

Even so, do not expect to see a totally unspoilt town. Chiang Mai changed a long time ago when the steady flow of admirers demanded an increase in hotels, guest houses, condominiums and shopping arcades. Still, for those in search of something a little different and who do not expect everything to be authentic, it still justifies the title 'Rose of the North', and is the most vibrant and convivial town in Thailand.

Legendary past

The Thais were latecomers to Chiang Mai. It was the Mons and the Lawa who first controlled the region through a string of principalities that lasted well into the 13th century.

Then came the turn of a Lanna chieftain named King Mengrai. Legend has it that he was riding along the banks of the Ping River in pursuit of an elephant when he noticed two white sambar deer, two white barking deer and five mice. Taking this as an auspicious sign, he founded the city of Chiang Mai on this precise spot and then went on to expand the Kingdom of Lanna until it stretched all the way from the northern frontier of the Sukhothai Kingdom to the southern provinces of China.

In 1556, Chiang Mai and much of the north fell to the Burmese who occupied the city on and off for almost 200 years. It was not until the late 1700s that the Thais regained control.

The latest people to leave a mark are property speculators, but even these are tied to ancient beliefs. Each property is started at an auspicious time to please the local spirits. And every year, festivals recall the legendary exploits of Lanna and the cultural integrity of a city which still quietly prides itself on its independence.

A place to wander

Chiang Mai offers much to see and do. The town is easily negotiated by using the red truck taxis (*songthaews*) that endlessly circulate around the town. Alternatively, you can explore on foot and hire a tricycle taxi or a *tuk tuk* when you are weary.

Thai Airways International has numerous daily flights from Bangkok to Chiang Mai that take 1 hour. Regular buses also leave the Northern Bus Terminal on Kampaengphet 2 Rd, Bangkok, taking 11 hours. The most pleasant means of transport is the overnight sleeper (13 hours) that leaves Bangkok's Hualamphong railway station in early evening, and gets you to the kingdom of Lanna at dawn.

Banyen Folk Art Museum

This charming little museum houses some of the finest antiques and woodcarvings. It was started more than 30 years ago by a young tribeswoman who has since become one of the best-known art collectors in the north. The leafy gardens and charming old traditional house are well worth a visit. *Off Wualai Rd. Tel: 0 5327 4007. Open: Fri–Wed 10am–4pm. Admission charge.*

Chiang Mai Zoo

Previously the private collection of Harold Young, an American working as an instructor with the Border Patrol Police, this is now Thailand's biggest zoo. It has about 500 species and a beautiful open-air bird sanctuary. *In a pretty area some 6km (4 miles) from town and best visited on the way to the mountain-top temple of Doi Suthep. Tel: 0 5322 1179. Open: daily 8am–5pm. Admission charge.*

Cultural Centre

Made from reconstructed tribal houses, the centre is the place to go for northern-style banqueting and dances. You can also enjoy the *khantoke*-style dinners along with coachloads of other tourists. *On 185/3 Wualai Rd. Tel: 0 5320 2993. Open: nightly 7–9.30pm. Reserve in advance.*

National Museum

A vast Buddha's head, believed to have been part of one of the biggest bronzes ever cast in Thailand, is the chief attraction of Chiang Mai's National Museum. There are other things to see, such as a massive Buddha footprint made from wood and mother-of-pearl, terracottas and ceramics. Folk and hill-tribe arts and crafts are exhibited on the upper floor, along with the bed of the former prince of Chiang Mai. *North of Super Highway, to the northwest of town. Tel: 0 5322 1308. Open: Wed–Sun 9am–4pm. Admission charge.*

A large Burmese python at the Chiang Mai Zoo

Night Bazaar

Bangkok's pride at night may be Patpong, but Chiang Mai attracts just as many visitors. The so-called Night Bazaar consists of the three-storey mock-Tudor Chiang Mai Plaza and the Ying Ping Bazaar. Their combined boutiques sell everything from high fashion to tribal costume, antiques, pots, lacquerware, jewellery and leather. Outside, on the roadside, are stalls selling camera film, painted beetles, bracelets, and fake designer T-shirts and watches, while nearby there are hundreds of sizzling foodstalls. Remember to bargain. *Chang Khlan Rd. Open: 6pm–midnight.*

San Kamphaeng Road

The 15-km (9-mile) stretch of tarmac that leads east of Chiang Mai to San Kamphaeng has become the biggest handicrafts market in the country. It is lined with emporia selling everything from silver and silk to woodcarvings and lacquerware. This is the place to stock up on presents and, more than anything, to watch village arts which are now disappearing. You can see silk being made from silkworms fed on mulberry leaves, lacquerware being sprayed

individually, and umbrellas painted by hand. There is no charge for browsing and it is not necessary to tip. Sometimes you can even order specially made items

Chiang Mai

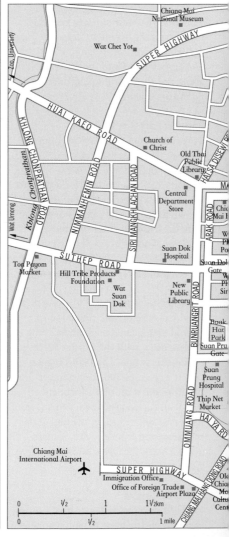

A treasure trove of handicrafts – painting a fan

that will be shipped back home for you.

It is best to arrive early, as it becomes crowded by the afternoon. There are plenty of restaurants or shops for snacks or ice cream in the vicinity.

To the east of Chiang Mai along Highway 1006, reached by bus from Charoen Muang Rd, or by tuk tuk.

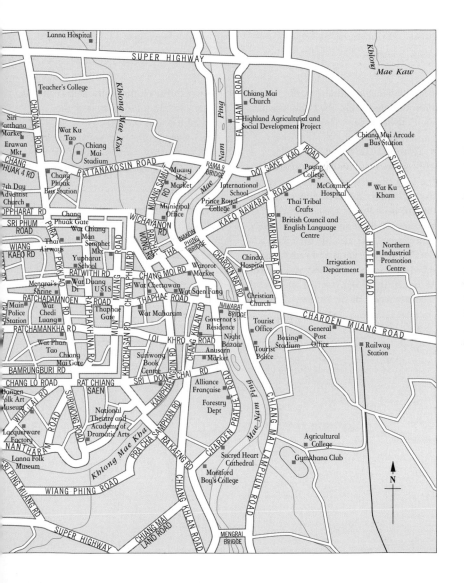

Walk: Chiang Mai's Thaphae Road

This walk takes you on a stroll through Chiang Mai's famous markets and temples and to the popular night bazaar on Chiang Khlan Road.
Allow 1½ hours.

Begin at Thaphae Gate opposite Ratchadamneon Rd. Walk east towards the Ping River down Thaphae Rd.

1 Thaphae Gate

This was one of five gates constructed in the 13th century, under King Mengrai, to defend his capital. Thaphae was said to have been built by 90,000 men working 24-hour shifts. Unfortunately, that did not stop the Burmese knocking down the walls, gates and ramparts when they invaded the city in the early 18th century. What is left is a modern reconstruction of the original; however,

it is worth the climb up the steps from where you can look down over the moated heart of the old city.
Turn down Thaphae Rd, walking away from the centre for around 200m (656ft) until you reach Wat Maharam on your right.

2 Wat Maharam

Although not one of Chiang Mai's better known temples, Wat Maharam does have a certain charm. It also shows the characteristic architectural shifts in style from the older Burmese *viharn* (temple hall) and *chedi* (pagoda) to the newer

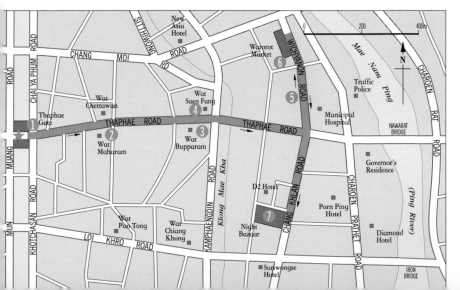

Lanna *bot* (main building). Running parallel to the *wat* is a quiet *soi* (alley), where you will hear the sound of birds and see some of the traditional old wooden houses.

Leave Wat Maharam and continue right down Thaphae Rd for 300m (984ft). On the right you will see Wat Bupparam.

3 Wat Bupparam

Built during the 15th century, and renovated in the 18th century, Wat Bupparam is one of the finest examples of Lanna architecture, with its five-headed *naga* snakes, Lanna-style roof and Burmese arches. Note the tiny old wooden *viharn* with its delicate engravings and, next door, a holy well whose waters are used for bathing the king.

Leave Wat Bupparam, turn right along Thaphae Rd, and walk 50m (164ft). Wat Saen Fang is on your left.

4 Wat Saen Fang

An oasis of calm in the midst of busy Thaphae Road, Wat Saen Fang incorporates part of the second ring of city walls. Inside is a tall Burmese-style *chedi* and some cannons once used to defend the city. On the windows there are beautiful golden engravings, showing scenes from the epic Ramayana and from the Jataka (life of Buddha) tales. On the door are depicted animals bringing water and honey to the meditating Buddha.

Leave Wat Saen Fang, turn left down Thaphae Rd, and continue for 300m (984ft) past stalls selling amulets and wooden Buddha images. Turn left down Wichyanon Rd.

5 Wichyanon Road

One of the most charming parts of the town, with narrow alleys, old houses and shops. This is a good place to buy silver bracelets and leather belts, or to wander into the Chinese gold shops.

Walk along Wichyanon Rd and bear left. After around 250m (820ft) you will reach the covered Warorot Market.

6 Warorot Market

The locals' treasure trove, Warorot is Chiang Mai's most authentic market, selling flowers, clothes, toys and, occasionally, delightful wooden bird cages. If you want to explore the fascinating side streets, just hire one of the tricycle taxis parked along the edge of the street.

Retrace your steps to Thaphae Rd and cross over to continue down Chang Khlan Rd for 300m (984ft). On the right you will see the Viang Ping Night Bazaar.

7 Night Bazaar

The three-floor emporium on Chiang Khlan Road is Chiang Mai's most popular shopping spot, stocking almost every sort of antique, cloth and trinket known to Thailand. Hill-tribe artefacts are attractive buys and make ideal souvenirs. Look out for the little metal weights, in the shape of elephants and birds, on sale as opium measures. Many of the antiques here are smuggled over the border from Myanmar. Although most of the stalls are only active from 6pm onwards, there are always a few that are open all day to attract tourist custom. As usual, bargain vigorously.

From the night bazaar, you can get a tuk tuk or songthaew (truck taxi) to take you back to Thaphae Gate.

Tricycle tour: Chiang Mai's walled city

This takes you on a gentle tour around the heart of old Chiang Mai and to the temples that were once the centre of city life. It starts from Suan Dok Gate.
Allow 1½ hours.

Hire one of the city's numerous tricycle taxis to take you on a circuit inside the city walls. The first stop is Wat Phra Singh, which lies at the intersection of Ratchadamnoen and Singharat Rds.

1 Wat Phra Singh
Built in the 14th century, Wat Phra Singh is best known as the residence of the famous Buddha Phra Singh, a statue said to have been brought from Sri

Lanka many centuries ago. Its head was stolen in 1922, but you can still see the replica. Inside the *viharn* (temple hall) is a collection of faded murals showing northern and Lanna customs, while outside is a charming 14th-century library.

Leaving the temple, turn right then second left down Ratchamankha Rd. After 500m (1,640ft), turn left down Phra Pokklao Rd where you will see Wat Chedi Luang.

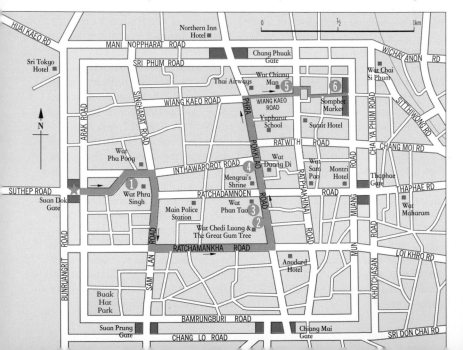

2 Wat Chedi Luang

Until a great earthquake shook the very foundations of the temple in 1545, the massive *chedi* (pagoda) of Wat Chedi Luang dwarfed all others. It was built by King Saen Muang Mai (1385–1401) and at one stage contained the famous Emerald Buddha (now in Bangkok's Grand Palace). Inside the *bot* (main hall) you can make merit by putting gold leaf on the statue of Luangpoowaen, a well-known *bhikkhu* (monk).

Walk out of the temple into the gardens and you will see a vast gum tree tied with a ribbon around its trunk.

3 The Great Gum Tree

This is the most famous and valued piece of wood in all Chiang Mai. Legend has it that as long as the tree stands, the town of Chiang Mai will thrive. Under the gum tree is the city pillar housed in a small building. It is customary to make a *wai* (greeting) or leave an offering of a wooden elephant or jasmine bouquet for the resident spirits.

Leave the temple compound and turn left. Continue for 50m (164ft) past Wat Phan Tao, a small wooden temple with beautiful stuccoed and gilded decorations. A short distance further on, you will reach a crossroads and Mengrai's Shrine.

4 Mengrai's Shrine

The small, gilded shrine that nestles on the intersection of Ratchadamnoen and Phra Pokklao Road recalls the great man who founded the city of Chiang Mai in 1296. Mengrai, according to popular legend, had it built in less than three years before going on to expand the kingdom of Lanna. Too great a man to suffer a normal fate, he was reputedly killed by lightning in 1311. Offerings of joss sticks are left in his memory.

From Mengrai's Shrine, continue straight for 800m (2,625ft) past Yupharat School (which occupies the site of the former palace) and turn right down Wiang Kaeo Rd, also known as Phra Pokklao Lane. About 200m (656ft) further down, you will see Wat Chiang Man on the left.

5 Wat Chiang Man

Reputedly the oldest *wat* in town, Wat Chiang Man is also one of the most delightful, with its quiet atmosphere and fragrant teak-wood monks' quarters. The temple is especially famous for the Phra Setang Khamani (Crystal Buddha), a statue said to have the power to bring rain. Equally potent is said to be the Phra Sila (Marble Buddha), a figure that was brought from India about 1,000 years ago.

Leave Wat Chiang Man, turn left, and cross over Ratphakhinai Rd. Somphet Market is situated at the end on Mun Muang Rd.

6 Somphet Market (Talaht Somphet)

One of Chiang Mai's lesser-known markets, this has delicious food stalls and colourful flowers. Try a *somtam* made with grated mango, lemon and garlic: add a little chilli, and feel the temperature rise. Afterwards, wander down the little alleys that sell exotic fruits, grilled fish and kebabs.

From Somphet Market, catch a tuk tuk or songthaew (truck taxi) home, or explore some of the surrounding area.

Chiang Mai's temples

Within the vicinity of Chiang Mai lie more than 300 temples, almost all of them still in use. Those listed here can easily be seen together or in small doses, as befits the mood. For a tricycle tour, see page 76. Alternatively, catch a day-tour organised by a big hotel.

Monumental Wat Ku Tao

Wat Chedi Luang
The temple was built in 1401 and later enlarged to a height of 86m (282ft). An earthquake in 1545 left the *chedi* in ruins, but it has now been impressively restored.
On Phra Pokklao Rd, near the intersection with Ratchamankha Rd. Open: daily 8am–5pm. Free admission.

Wat Chiang Man
Chiang Mai's oldest temple built around AD 1296, Wat Chiang Man, housing the ancient and invaluable Buddha image Phra Kaeo Khao, was founded by Mengrai, the man who established the great Kingdom of Lanna and subsequently died there, struck by a bolt of lightning. Two figures are particularly revered and are believed to have supernatural powers.
Off Ratphakhinai Rd within the walled city. Open: daily 9am–5pm. Free admission.

Wat Chet Yot
Wat Chet Yot, known as the 'Temple of Seven Spires', was built in the 15th century, during the reign of King Tilokaraja, to recall the great Mahabodhi temple in Bodh Gaya (India), where Buddha achieved enlightenment. This is one of the most striking and important of the town's temples. Inside the larger *chedi* (pagoda) are the ashes of King Tilokaraja, and outside the two sacred bo trees are said to have been brought from the original one in the Kingdom of Sakyas in present-day Nepal.
On the Super Highway, off Huai Kaeo Rd. Open: daily 8am–5pm. Free admission.

Wat Ku Tao
This is one of the most delightful temples you will come across, with its *chedi* shaped like five melons, intricately decorated with pieces of coloured porcelain. The structure, dating from 1613, is believed to represent five alms bowls of Buddhist monks which symbolise five Lord Buddhas. Note the striking sculptures on the outer walls.
North of the moat near the Chiang Mai Sports Stadium, off Rattanakosin Road. Free admission.

Wat Phra Singh
The 14th-century Wat Phra Singh became the residence for one of the kingdom's most famous statues when a cart carrying the precious figure broke down on its way from Lampang. The Phra Singh image has since lost its head when it was carted off by thieves in

1922, but its replacement remains.
*At the intersection of Ratchadamnoen
and Singharat rds. Open: daily
8am–5pm. Free admission.*

Wat Suan Dok

This is the perfect spot to be at sunset,
with the three ancient *chedis* framed
against the distant hills. Wat Suan Dok
(Flower Garden Temple) was built by
King Ku Na in 1383, within the pleasure
gardens of the monarchs of Lanna and
it contains a large, 500-year-old bronze
image of Buddha in Chiang Saen style.
Most of the royals of Chiang Mai are
buried in the cemetery adjoining the
temple. Among the several *chedis*, one is
said to contain an important relic of the
Buddha brought here by an elephant.
*Off Cherng Doy Rd, south of Suthep Rd,
on the western outskirts of town.
Open: daily 8am–5pm. Free admission.*

Wat Umong

Away from the other temples, in the
relative quiet of the edge of town, Wat
Umong is more like a monastic retreat
than a traditional *wat*. It was built
by King Mengrai for a famous monk
who could not stay in the city
because he wanted to practise Lord
Buddha's teachings in a peaceful
environment.

Inside the grounds are cells for
meditation, and attached to the trees are
tablets advising people that 'today is
better than two tomorrows'.

In the past, several foreign monks
have resided here.
*In the western outskirts, reached by taking
the Suthep Rd. Shortly beyond the
junction with Khlong Chonprathan Rd,
take the turning to the left, signposted to
the* wat*, which is reached after 1km
(¹/₂ mile). Free admission.*

Wat Phra Singh contains some fine buildings as well as precious statues

CHIANG MAI ENVIRONS
Doi Inthanon

Thailand's tallest mountain cannot compare with any in the Himalayas, but at 2,565m (8,415ft) it still offers fine views of the surrounding national park 482sq km (186sq miles). From along the steep road that runs all the way from the park entrance to the top of Doi Inthanon, walks can be taken to caves and tribal villages, although you should get maps or hire guides from the park headquarters. Birdwatchers are well rewarded, as the park has one of the highest populations of birdlife, including the rare, ashy-throated warbler, and the yellow-bellied flowerpecker.

On the way up, visit the Mae Klang Waterfall, signposted outside the park gates, and truly spectacular during the rainy months from August to November.

Doi Inthanon lies 80km (50 miles) southwest of Chiang Mai. Tours are generally the best way of seeing the park, since buses only go as far as Chom Thong, from where you will have to catch another to Mae Klang, and from there take a songthaew to Doi Inthanon. Alternatively, use private transport. Accommodation is available.

Doi Suthep

High up an exciting road that zigzags its way up the mountainside is the revered temple of Doi Suthep, which dates from 1383. Legend has it that the temple was established at the spot on the summit where one of the king's own white elephants, fleeing from the palace, climbed, trumpeted three times, and died. Centuries later, pious volunteers constructed a road there, with people coming from as far as Lampang to contribute to the endeavours. You cannot, however, go all the way on four wheels. The road curves around near the base of the hill, and visitors must still either take the arduous 290-step climb up a *naga* staircase, or a four-minute ride on the mountain railway.

At the top is a monastery with bells and gold umbrellas, and rows of Buddhas marking the spot where important relics are encased. A clear day may give fine views of Chiang Mai.

15km (9 miles) west of Chiang Mai. Minibuses regularly leave from the Chang Phuak (White Elephant) Gate, on the northern edge of Chiang Mai's moat. Most people take tours.

Phu Phing Palace

Four kilometres (2¹/₂ miles) up the road from Doi Suthep is the Phu Phing Palace, the royal winter residence of the king, with its sumptuous gardens.

Open: Fri–Sun, except when the royal family is in residence.

Tribal Village of Ban Doi Pui

The tribal village of Ban Doi Pui is inhabited by the Hmong (or Meo), a minority group characterised by their colourful costumes and handicrafts. This village provides little by way of authenticity, but it does give a sense of the colour and the traditions of the tribal society.

8km (5 miles) from Doi Suthep and 4km (2¹/₂ miles) from Phu Phing Palace. Trips to the Hmong village are combined with tours to Doi Suthep.

Lampang

An old timber-cutting town and a former staging post on the journey north, during the 7th century Lampang was an outlying settlement of the Haripunchai empire. These days its biggest claim to fame is that horse-drawn carts remain a popular form of transport.

One sight not to be missed is Wat Phra Kaeo Don Tao, the temple near the banks of Wang River, which is once said to have housed the famous Emerald Buddha. Smaller, typically Burmese temples, such as Wat Sri Chum and Wat Pha Fang, are also worth exploring. Another gem for the real temple fanatic is the beautiful Wat Phra That Lampang Luang, some 16km (10 miles) to the southwest of the town, sporting fine bronzes and woodwork, as well as an Emerald Buddha image said to have been cut from the same stone as the one now in Bangkok.

99km (61 1/2 miles) south of Chiang Mai. Buses run from the Chiang Mai Arcade station, taking 1 1/2 hours. The town is also on the main railway line linking Bangkok and Chiang Mai.

The revered temple of Doi Suthep

Lamphun

A 30-minute drive from Chiang Mai, along a road lined with majestic trees, will bring you to another old historical city, once the capital of the great kingdom of Haripunchai. Lamphun was founded in 660 by Queen Chamadevi and remained the capital until 1281, when the empire fell under the sovereignty of King Mengrai, monarch of the Lanna dynasty.

No visitor to the town should miss the temple complex of Wat Phra That Haripunchai, on Highway II. Founded in 1044, the temple has two fine bronze Buddha statues. It is topped by a 46-m (151-ft) golden *chedi* (pagoda), and also bears two ornamental lions.

A couple of other sights deserve a mention. Wat Ku Kut (commonly known as Wat Chamadevi), on the western side of town towards San Pa Tong, dates from the 8th century, although some of the buildings are modern. Opposite Wat Phra That Haripunchai, there is also the small national museum (*open: Wed–Sun 8.30am–4pm*), with a collection of sculptures from the Dvaravati,

Haripunchai, Lanna and Rattanakosin periods.

If you have time, take a *songthaew* (truck taxi) to the town of Pa Sang, which lies 11km (7 miles) to the southwest. This is famed for its *longans* (a fruit resembling a lychee), its handicrafts and, above all, its beautiful women.
26km (16 miles) south of Chiang Mai, reached by regular bus from Lamphun Rd near Nawarat Bridge.

Mae Sa Valley

Everything that tourists associate with the north is on offer in Mae Sa, a lush valley that has become a showpiece of local cultural and natural attractions: orchid cultivation, elephants, butterfly farms, snake farms, waterfalls – they are all to be found here, along with quaint resorts, and hill-tribe centres.

The place is especially good for children who wish to see things without too much traipsing around. It is, however, thoroughly commercialised and has to be taken with a pinch of salt.
15km (9 miles) north of Chiang Mai. Day tours or private trans-port are best, since buses only go as far as Mae Rim.

ORCHIDS GALORE

Thailand's most famous flower is the orchid. The kingdom grows some 1,000 different varieties, making it one of the most prolific producers in the world.

Some of the most famous orchids are 'Queen Sirikit' (*Paphiopedium ascocenda*) and 'Miss Udorn Sunshine', both renowned for their subtle fragrance and elegance. The best place to see them is in the orchid farms around Chiang Mai and in the Mae Sa Valley. Thailand's favourite flower can be appreciated in Bangkok, in the early morning markets and stalls. Its export worldwide has made it a familiar item in flower shops everywhere.

Mae Taeng

The name of Mae Taeng is associated with Thailand's most beloved four-legged animal: the *chang*, or elephant, which was, until recently, found not only in the forests of the north, but also in the king's palace in Bangkok where it was frequently consulted on important matters of state. The elephants of Mae Taeng are, however, just reminders of a sight once common throughout the country, when they were used to drag logs to the river, to be floated downstream. The use of elephants has declined over the centuries and they are now used mainly for tourist displays. At daily shows, however, mahouts show the skill and adaptability of their massive steeds, and elephant rides provide visitors with the feel and smell of these obliging beasts. Organised raft trips can be taken through the leafy woodlands around the park.

60km (37 miles) north of Chiang Mai. Day trips are organised by travel agencies. Alternatively, catch a bus leaving the Chang Phuak Terminal on Chotana Rd, direction Fang, and ask for the Elephant Farm & Training Centre. Open: daily 9am–12.30pm. Admission charge.

Working elephants enjoy their daily bath

Hill tribes

They live in the northern hills, high up near the borders in the area known as the Golden Triangle, the wilderness of land that lies at the point where the borders of Laos, Thailand and Myanmar meet. They wear bright, colourful clothes and worship the spirits of the hills and the rains.

The hill-tribe population of Thailand numbers approximately 700,000, and is made up of the Akha, Karen, Lahu, Lisu, Hmong (Meo) and Mien. Each tribe comes from a different ancestral home, wears a different costume, and has distinctive attitudes towards the spirits, to marriage, to sickness and to wealth.

Traditionally, these people tilled the soil, growing opium, maize and

potatoes high up in the barren hills and migrating when the soil was turned over to fallow. Many came from over the Thai border, crossing freely between countries, settling on the fringes of northern Thailand, and moving on.

With time, modern lifestyles have gradually made inroads into the tribal communities. Some tribespeople have become farmers, having moved down to the plains, while others have given up their tribal clothes for jeans, T-shirts and a life in the city.

Even so, the majority of tribespeople still preserve at least some of their traditions, eking out an existence that appears, from the outside, to be idyllic, though in reality it is a hard life tied to the soil, the family spirits and the home.

A word of advice: ensure that when making a visit to see one of the hill tribes, you take an organised tour with a recognised travel agency.

The different faces of Thailand: Facing page above: Hmong woman and son; below: Lahu tribesman. This page left: the long-necked Karen; above & below: an Akha girl and elder

An opulent Buddha image at the rear centre of the Wat Phra Singh, Chiang Rai

Chiang Rai

The northernmost capital of Chiang Rai is one of the oldest towns in Thailand. Now, despite the many modern hotels catering to the growing influx of tourists, there is still something rather provincial about the place. The town is 182km (113 miles) north of Chiang Mai. Nearby are the towns of Doi Mae Salong, Mae Sai, Chiang Saen and the Golden Triangle.

There are only a limited number of sights, but Chiang Rai's biggest attractions lie in the surrounding countryside, with the town's hotels and restaurants merely serving those who begin or end their journey there.

Most people come here for trekking trips, ranging from one-day packages in buses to five days on elephants and rafts. You only need walk down the main street to find something tailored to your price range and desired degree of comfort.

A wild elephant

If it were not for an elephant that ran wild, Chiang Rai might never have been established at all. As legend recalls, it was only this that attracted King Mengrai to the auspicious site where he founded the city in 1262.

For a short spell, Chiang Rai served as the capital of the Lanna kingdom, but it was rapidly eclipsed by the growth of Chiang Mai. It fell to the Burmese in the 16th century and became a jungle backwater close to the border areas, where the tribes and the drug smugglers reigned supreme.

Thus it remained until the present day, when Chiang Rai began to expand as Chiang Mai began to feel the strains of expansion.

Chiang Rai is reached from Chiang Mai by river (see below) by regular buses, taking 4 hours, or by aeroplane, taking 40 minutes.

River journey

One of the greatest highlights of a visit to Chiang Rai may well prove to be the journey there and back from Chiang Mai, since part of the trip is by boat and passes through some of the most spectacular scenery in the region.

To do the trip you must catch a bus or *songthaew* to Tha Ton, a little settlement five hours due north of Chiang Mai, on the banks of the Kok River. From here, boats leave at around noon daily for the five-hour trip to Chiang Rai. The long-tailed boats are fast and uncomfortable and have no toilets. Any short-term discomforts, however, are made up for by the countryside and the views of hills, villages and countless water buffalo. Rafts can also be rented for a slower, three-day journey to Chiang Rai, although you are well advised to make advance reservations.

Temples

Chiang Rai's most famous temple is the 13th-century Wat Phra Kaeo on Trairat Road, home to a model of the Emerald Buddha. To the west of Wat Phra Kaeo, situated on a small hill, is Wat Doi Tong, with fine views of the Kok River and the distant hills beyond.
Open: daily 8.30am–6pm.
Free admission.

Tribes and elephants

One popular side trip is to the tribal village of **Ban Ruammit** on the banks of the Kok River. The Karen tribespeople here are no strangers to tourism. Most visitors enjoy the elephant rides and the scenery on the way. A long-tailed boat leaves daily from the pier near the Dusit Resort; the journey takes one hour, but you must return by minibus.

Further afield are the towns of Mae Chan, 32km (20 miles) north, and Doi Mae Salong, 67km (41^1/2 miles) northwest, far enough off to get a real feel of the isolated countryside, but near enough for luxury and a touch of homely comforts. Both can be reached by bus and organised tours.

Take an early-morning trip down the Kok River to get away from it all

The Golden Triangle

No other area in Thailand conjures up such images as the Golden Triangle, the evocative-sounding region that lies to the north of Chiang Rai at the point where the great rivers of Mekong and **Ban Sop Ruak** meet to form the apex of Thailand, Laos and Myanmar.

It is little wonder the region gained its legendary infamy. Since the 1960s, it has become the largest supplier of opium in the world, second only to Afghanistan. It is also home to a variety of rebel armies which finance their continuing insurgencies through the production of heroin and methamphetamines.

Pinpointing the exact location of the triangle was largely irrelevant until the tourist authorities ingeniously found a spot for it. Now there is a big plaque opposite a sandbank at Ban Sop Ruak, a range of over-priced boat trips, and countless stalls selling Golden Triangle T-shirts. Most people who come here are invariably disappointed. It is far better to explore the surrounding countryside or the thriving towns of Mae Sai and Chiang Saen. *The Golden Triangle is centred on the town of Ban Sop Ruak, some 40km (25 miles) north of Chiang Rai.*

Mae Sai

The main town nearest to the official Golden Triangle is Mae Sai. It lies about as far north as you can go in Thailand. The town hugs

OPIUM

*P*apaver somniferum is the Latin name of the poppy that produces one of the world's most dangerous drugs. Opium is found in the resin of the poppy, extracted by hand and turned into heroin in refineries along the Thai border.

Every year more than 800 tonnes comes over from the Golden Triangle, shipped, flown and smuggled across the world. Some of it is sold in the big cities of Thailand and some is used by the local tribes, a few of whom are addicts.

While recent efforts have led to the suppression of opium cultivation in Thailand, the flow of drugs from the bordering countries shows no sign of abating.

The Mekong at the Golden Triangle of Myanmar (left) and Laos (right)

the banks of the Mae Sai River, a jumble of wooden houses, concrete shops and corrugated shacks bisected by a long road, and an austere concrete bridge leading to Myanmar.

Every day, from 6am to 6pm, the bridge is the scene of frenzied shopping, for this is the main border crossing. Bring a camera and take some time.

Afterwards, try shopping for gems or woven Burmese carpets or herbs in the market, or along the main road which leads down from the bridge. Many of the beautiful *sequens* (mother-of-pearl buttons) and puppets are of such quality that they draw buyers from as far afield as Bangkok.

But where there are bargains, there are inevitable fakes, and many jewel buyers may find themselves bearing away little more than coloured pieces of glass. *61km (38 miles) north of Chiang Rai and reached by frequent buses, taking*

1½ hours. A VIP bus leaves daily from Bangkok (contact local travel agents).

Chiang Saen

Chiang Saen has something of history, a little bit of intrigue, and a great deal of calm. It lies just a few steps from the border with Laos, on the Mekong, and 30km (18¹/₂ miles) from Mae Chan.

Founded in the 14th century by the Mengrai dynasty, the town went on to become the centre of one of the earliest northern principalities. Reminders of those days can still be found in the old moat that surrounds the town, the fascinating museum situated near the city gate, and Wat Pa Sak (Teak Forest Temple) with its magnificent stuccoed *chedi* (pagoda) which predates the town. *58km (36 miles) northeast of Chiang Rai. Chiang Saen can be reached by bus from Chiang Rai and Mae Sai. Museum open: Wed–Sun 9am–4pm except holidays.*

Potent opium is obtained from these beautiful and innocuous-looking poppies

Mae Hong Son

Mae Hong Son (City of Mists) lies in a deep valley surrounded by hills, at the end of a staggeringly beautiful 8-hour, 349km (217 mile) drive from Chiang Mai, or a more bearable 30-minute flight. Situated northwest of Chiang Mai, Mae Hong Son is all about a sense of isolation, green hills and misty mornings. Nearby towns are **Mae Sariang**, 168km (104 miles) south, **Pai**, 102km (63 miles) east and **Soppong**, 57km (35.4 miles) northeast. The town was only accessible by elephant until the early 20th century.

Indeed, until a few years ago, there was not even an airport. Now Mae Hong Son has the advantage of road and air connections, as well as the comfort of good hotels.

Its few main streets pack in a fair amount of things to see, including temples, a picturesque lake and a morning market. The real tonic is the scenic back-drop, the distant views, and the mountain air.

If you are coming between November and February, remember to bring a sweater. Mae Hong Son can be bitterly cold, with temperatures at night falling to 5°C (40°F).

Buses to Mae Hong Son leave from Chiang Mai's Arcade Bus Station; those going via Pai taking 7 to 8 hours, while those taking the more difficult route, via Mae Sariang, take 8 to 9 hours. A better alternative is the 30-minute Thai Airways flight.

Morning market

You can still occasionally see some of the local tribespeople visiting the morning market. Try to get there at dawn because by 8am most people have packed up and gone home. *Behind the Mae Tee Hotel on Panetwattana Rd.*

Soppong and Pai

For the adventurous, trips can be made to the beautiful **Tham Lot cave temple**, 68km (42 miles) away near Soppong, or to the small mountain village of Pai, which lies 45km (28 miles) further east. Both are situated in beautiful countryside, and are easily reached by bus.

Alternatively, there are now several organisations renting out motorbikes, in some cases even jeeps. However, if you hire a bike, be very careful; the terrain

Famous bronze Buddha image in Wat Hua Wiang

is difficult, and foreigners with bandaged ankles are numerous!

Tham Pla

This is Mae Hong Son's most popular and easily reached sight. Tham Pla (Fish Cave) contains large and overweight carp fed on peanuts by visitors hoping to win merit. Some people find it disappointing, but children love it.
18km (11 miles) north of town on the road to Pai.

Trekking and tribes

Another of Mae Hong Son's specialities is the trip to the long-necked tribe, known as the Padaung, who live in a village close to the Myanmar border, reached by daily tours.

Mae Hong Son is also a good place to arrange trekking, or to go elephant riding, or rafting along the Pai River. Enquire at travel agents.

Wat Chong Khlong and Wat Chong Kam

The most picturesque of Mae Hong Son's monasteries, they are home to over 30 carved-wood statues brought from Myanmar around 1860. Located on the banks of the charming Nong Chongkham Lake, they are best visited in the morning when the lake is veiled by mist.

Off Chumnan Sathit Rd to the south of town. Both open: daily. Free admission.

Wat Hua Wiang

This is an incongruous wooden temple that would look more at home in Myanmar than in Thailand. It contains a highly venerated bronze Buddha statue which was cast in Myanmar.
On Panetwattana Rd next to the market. Open: daily 8am–6pm. Free admission.

Wat Phra That Doi Kong Mu

The hilltop War Phra That Doi Kong Mu dominates the provincial city. Constructed by Phraya Singhanetracha, the first ruler of Mae Hong Son, it boasts fabulous views of the city.

The pretty little town of Mae Hong Son

Sukhothai

The 'Dawn of Happiness', the chapter of history which ushered in one of Thailand's greatest civilisations, began in the town of Sukhothai, the ancient kingdom that lies almost midway between Bangkok and Chiang Mai. To the east is the major provincial town of Phitsanulok, 50km (31 miles) away, and to the west are the towns of Tak, 80km (50 miles) away, and Mae Sot, 160km (99 miles) away.

The Sukhothai period lasted less than 150 years (from 1238 to 1376), but is considered a golden age of Thai art and religion, producing some of the greatest monuments. Historical artefacts have shown that Thai culture originated in Sukhothai, most particularly the Thai language and alphabet.

These ruins are spread over an area of 45sq km (17sq miles) and are best seen by taking a tour of the historical park (*see p94*) or by hiring a guide to point out and elaborate on the most important monuments.

427km (265 miles) north of Bangkok. Sukhothai can be reached by bus from Bangkok's Northern Bus Terminal on Kampaengphet 2 Rd. Alternatively, catch a train from Bangkok's Hualamphong railway station to Phitsanulok, the nearest provincial town, from where it is a short hour's journey to Sukhothai by bus.

Historical Park

Almost all the major sights are situated within the historical park, 13km (8 miles) west of the town. Three temples, in particular, should not be missed.

Wat Mahathat is the most important temple. Built in the 13th century, it contains massive Buddha images which preside over a complex of columns. Wat Si Chum is situated outside the northwest corner of the city and contains a gigantic seated Buddha, measuring over 11m (36ft) across from knee to knee. Wat Si Sawai is a beautiful Khmer-style temple built in the 13th century; it is surrounded by a picturesque moat.

Outside the city walls, some 3km (2 miles) to the west, are the temples of Wat Saphin Hin and Wat Chang Rob – wilder, less visited, and best seen by hiring a bicycle.

THE PERFECT BUDDHA

The most beautiful, serene and perfect Buddhas were those that evolved during the Sukhothai period. They are distinguished by their broad shoulders, elongated limbs and delicate oval faces. Many of the Buddhas are made from stucco and bronze, cast with unsurpassed craftsmanship. So meticulously and carefully have they been crafted that they emanate an air of radiant calm, something that few artistic pieces can aspire to.

Another sight worth a visit is the **Ramkamhaeng Museum**, containing a replica of the famous Ramkamhaeng inscription: 'There is rice in the fields. There are fish in the water. Those who want to laughcan laugh, those who want to cry can cry.'

Ramkamhaeng Museum: 13km (8 miles) from new Sukhothai, easily reached by songthaew. Open: daily 9am–4pm. Admission charge.

Si Satchanalai

An hour's drive north from Sukhothai is the old walled city of Si Satchanalai. Wilder, more compact and, for the most part, less visited, it contains a wealth of temples, albeit on a smaller scale than in Sukhothai.

Wat Chang Lom is Si Satchanalai's most impressive monument. It dates from the 13th century and contains a large *chedi* (pagoda) raised on a base decorated with 39 elephant buttresses.

Wat Chedi Chet Thaew is situated opposite Wat Chang Lom. This 14th-century temple houses seven rows of *chedis* said to contain the ashes of the city's rulers. Wat Kah Phanom Phloeng is reached via a steep flight of stairs. The temple showcases a seated Buddha, and has fine views of the ruins below.

The old walled city is situated 5km (3 miles) south of the new town of Si Satchanalai. It can be reached by a bus that leaves Sukhothai every hour. Open: daily 8.30am–4.30pm. Admission charge.

Ban Ko Noi

Outside the walled city, near the town of Ban Ko Noi, you can visit the kilns which produced some of Thailand's earliest and most beautiful pottery. Such was the value of the grey-green Sawankalok porcelain, that examples have been discovered as far afield as Borneo and Sumatra.

4km (2¹/₂ miles) north of Si Satchanalai. Open: daily 9am–4pm. Admission charge.

Ancient Wat Chang Lom in Si Satchanalai

By bike: Around Sukhothai

This tour takes you around some of the most spectacular and least-visited ruins at Sukhothai, the first great kingdom of the Thais.
Allow 4 hours.

Start at the market outside the historical park, hire a bicycle from one of the shops on the main road, and head to Ramkamhaeng National Museum, signposted to the left just off the roundabout.

1 Ramkamhaeng National Museum
Built in 1960 in memory of Sukhothai's greatest king, the Ramkamhaeng National Museum contains a superb collection of Sukhothai sculpture brought from Sukhothai, Si Satchanalai and Kamphaeng Phet. Note the magnificent 14th-century 'walking' Buddha just inside the entrance, the famous inscription, and the stucco decorations which have become the hallmark of Thailand's most graceful period of art (*see pp92–3*).
Leave the museum and, at the roundabout, turn left into the historical park. Wat Mahathat is 250m (820ft) further on to the right.

2 Wat Mahathat and the Royal Palace
This is the largest and, for many, the most beautiful, of Sukhothai's temples. Built in the 13th century by Sri Indrathit, 'Father of Dignitaries', it sits among lotus-filled ponds, has 198 *chedis*

(pagodas), and was formerly the home of a vast, seated bronze Buddha.
From Wat Mahathat return to the intersection, and take the minor road almost directly opposite. Take the first left, and 350m (1,148ft) further on, you will see Wat Sa Si.

3 Wat Sa Si
Situated on two connected islands, Wat Sa Si (Temple of the Splendid Pond) contains a monumental seated Buddha gazing peacefully out past rows of columns to the water beyond.
From Wat Sa Si retrace your steps and turn left at the signpost for San Luang Gate, which lies 600m (1,969ft) further on.

4 San Luang Gate
The northern gate and entry to the city, San Luang (House of the Royal Spirit) forms part of the earthen ramparts that originally surrounded Sukhothai.
Continue along the road past the San Luang Gate and you will come to Wat Phra Phai Luang, situated 500m (1,640ft) further on the left.

5 Wat Phra Phai Luang
Known as the Temple of the Great Wind, this is one of the city's oldest monasteries and was originally built by

the Khmers as a Hindu temple. Among the ruins, spread over a vast area of grass, you can still see the ramparts, surrounded by a moat, typical of the religious architecture of the time. Note the northern *prang* (spire), decorated with stucco Hindu and Buddhist figures. *Leave the* wat *and cycle around the moat. After 100m (388ft) turn left. 500m (1,640ft) further on, you will see the kilns at Tao Thuriang.*

6 Tao Thuriang (Potters' Kilns)

Excavations have so far brought to light 49 kilns, spread over an area of 3 hectares (7½ acres). These were first used before AD 1300, and produced a special kind of celadon (green-glazed ware), with pots distinguished by the imprint of a fish or flower on the base.

Leave Tao Thuriang, and continue for 1.3km (¾ mile) to Wat Si Chum, situated on the right.

7 Wat Si Chum

This *wat* is famed for its awesome Buddha housed within a massive square *mondop* (shrine). The image, known as Phra Achana or Venerable Buddha, is seated cross-legged. It is 11.3m (37ft) from knee to knee, 15m (39ft) tall, and is rumoured to have once halted a Burmese invasion. Inside the walls of the shrine, which are 3m (10ft) thick, is a secret passage, with a ceiling engraved with scenes from the Jataka tales. *Leave Wat Si Chum and continue along the road. At the next intersection, turn left back to the historical park. Return your cycle and catch a* songthaew *home.*

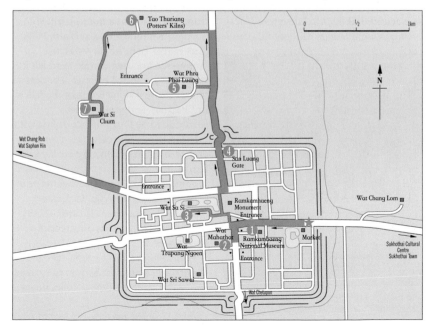

Northeast Thailand

KHORAT
(NAKHON RATCHASIMA)

The town that foreigners know of as Khorat lies 259km (161 miles) northeast of Bangkok at the entrance to the Khorat Plateau. The Thais call their town Nakhon Ratchasima.

The confusion over names, along with the lack of infrastructure and the rarity of English-speaking natives, are enough to put off all but the most persevering. That, however, can be part of the attraction. People do not come to Khorat to see the town; they come here to use it as the gateway to some of the greatest ruins in the country.

Even so, everyone passing through should try to visit the night market on Manat Road, as well as the statue of the famous Khun Ying Mo, the revered local who, during the reign of Rama III, saved the town from the Laotians. The statue is situated at the Chumpon Gate on the west side of town.

Nearby major towns are **Buriram** and **Surin**, 150km (93 miles) and 197km (122 miles) to the east respectively. **Khao Yai National Park** is 99km (61^1/$_2$ miles) to the west.
Trains run to Khorat 11 times a day from Hualamphong railway station in Bangkok, taking approximately 5 hours. In addition, regular buses leave from Bangkok's Northern Bus Terminal on Phahon Yothin Rd.

Ancient ruins of Phimai

One of the world's valued wonders, the 11th-century temple at Phimai has become a tourist attraction for good reason. It lies just an hour's journey north of Khorat by bus, and just 240km (149 miles) from Angkor Wat, the famous Cambodian temple to which it was once connected by road. The central *prasad* (tower) alone is one of the tallest in Thailand, and is elaborately surrounded by four porches etched with intricate sandstone carvings of *nagas* and *garudas*, the mythical guardians of the temple.

Although the temple reached its peak of glory during the reign of Angkor monarch Jayavarman VII (1181–1219), it fell into ruin and has only recently been restored.

From Phimai, most people take the chance to visit a giant banyan tree called Sai Ngam, situated 2km (1 mile) down the road.
60km (37 miles) northeast of Khorat.

The ruins of 11th-century Phimai where carvings demonstrate the artistry of the Khmer people

Buses leave the main bus station on Suranari Rd every 30 minutes during the day.

Muang Tam

This 10th-century temple is another beautiful example of Khmer architecture, with three ancient ponds within its walled compound. Muang Tam is less visited, wilder and surrounded by the true countryside of Isaan, a just reward for those who have made the effort to get there.
7km (4 miles) south of Phanom Rung.

Pak Thong Chai

Anyone coming to northeast Thailand should spend at least half a day exploring the region's two most famous commodities: silk and *mutmee*. Mutmee in particular is associated with the northeast, and is a unique form of tie-dyed silk in which the threads are tied according to the desired pattern before being dyed. Shops in Khorat sell fabulous quality silk. You can also watch the weavers at their looms in the town of Pak Thong Chai.
Pak Thong Chai lies 30km (18¹/₂ miles) to the southwest of Khorat. The town is reached by bus that leaves Khorat every 30 minutes.

Phanom Rung

Another fine example of Khmer architecture, Phanom Rung is solemnly perched on top of an extinct volcano. It is reached by a dramatic avenue paved with laterite, flanked by sandstone pillars, with ascending levels and three magnificent bridges carved with mythical beasts called *nagas*. The

The temple of Prasat Hin Phanom Rung

Khmers believed that the nearer to the sky a shrine was situated, the closer to the gods it would be. No wonder the shrine of Phanom Rung is considered especially sacred.
101km (63 miles) southeast of Khorat. You can take a bus from Khorat to Ban Ta Ko (bus terminal 2, bus No. 274) from where, with luck, you will catch a songthaew. A better bet is to take a tour.

The Khmers
From the 8th to the 11th century, vast areas of northeast Thailand were inhabited by the Khmers, the present-day Cambodians. Although they were gradually displaced by the Thais, they left behind them ruined temples dedicated to Hindu gods and to the Buddha, which combine a raw power, found in few other artistic periods in Thai history.

LOEI PROVINCE

The lure of Loei is its mountains, its waterfalls and its lush forest. The region, accessible only by a long road journey, is considered to be the Siberia of Thailand.

In reality, it is one of the undiscovered gems of the northeast, calm and quiet, with some of the greatest national parks in the country.

Loei town is situated 520km (323 miles) northeast of Bangkok. Buses leave the Northern Bus Terminal on Kampaengphet 2 Rd several times a day, and the journey takes 10 hours.

Chiang Khan

On the Mekong River, almost on the border with Laos, is the small town of Chiang Khan, set in a valley amid rolling hills. Downstream 5km (3 miles) are the spectacular **Kaeng Khut Khu Rapids**. The town is favoured for its relative isolation and pleasant scenery.

47km (29 miles) north of Loei town and can be reached by songthaew *from Loei bus station.*

Nong Khai

The most popular town in the northeast, Nong Khai owes this position as much to its accessibility by rail as to its delightful river setting and proximity to Laos.

Long, tree-lined boulevards stretch along the banks of the Mekong. From the cafés that dot the banks, you can watch boats leave for the tiny Laotian border village of Tha Dua. You can also eat French *baguette* (bread) in the markets and, at night, stare out at the twinkling lights of Vientiane, capital of the former French colony which fell to the Communists in 1975, now slowly re-emerging from its long, self-imposed isolation.

On the outskirts of the town, visit Wat Po Chai, site of the annual rocket festival, and the bizarre Brahmin complex of Wat Khaek, about 5km (3 miles) to the east.

614km (381$\frac{1}{2}$ miles) northeast of Bangkok. Trains leave Hualamphong station 4 times daily, taking 10 hours.

Buses run from the Northern Bus Terminal, Phahon Yothin Rd, taking 9 hours.

Phu Kradung

Sitting on a plateau 1,325m (4,347ft) high is

this weird and wonderful bell-shaped mountain that local people believe was made by spirits. Access to Phu Kradung is by a steep path that winds its way up the hill. Guides undertake the journey in two hours and often carry baggage.

From the top of the plateau, you may catch glimpses of wild pigs or giant squirrels and, if you are lucky, elephants. More common are the unparalleled views of the plateau from Pha Nok Aen at dawn, when it is shrouded in mist.

73km (45 miles) south of Loei. Daily buses run from Loei to Phu Kradung. Check with the tourist office before setting off. During the rainy months (Jul–Oct), the national park is closed.

Phu Luang Wildlife Sanctuary

Adventurous travellers can head for the Phu Luang Park, set high up on a plateau amid magnificent scenery southwest of Loei. It is a blend of tropical and colder forests, with abundant wildlife.

Ferryboats cross the river: some local people navigate the mighty Mekong many times a day

In the alternately wet and arid land that makes up the vast canvas of northeast Thailand, live the people of Isaan: the 20 million farmers, rice workers and traders who have made this their home. Poor, isolated, tied to their soil, they are the underprivileged of the kingdom. However, of late their plight has started to receive more attention in Thai political discourse, with government grants encouraging and sustaining rural development.

Many Isaan people are from Khmer stock or from Laos. Physically, they are quite notably different from the Thais, their skin darker, their physiques smaller and wirier. Linguistically, they speak a language more akin to Khmer or Laotian. For many of them, Bangkok is another world, and the next-door village as far as their travels will ever take them. For others, the search for better employment takes them further afield. Unfortunately, as it happens, many of them end up with the jobs that other Thais would not even consider.

Life in Isaan is based on the land. The farmers and rice workers start their long day before dawn, waking to the calls of the cockerels in the fields, farming rice and vegetables, enjoying a sleep during the midday sun, and continuing to work until sundown. Having returned home, the farmers will gather in their small village communities and enjoy a very strong white whisky (*lao khao*); play their traditional bamboo instrument called *khaen*; and enjoy local delicacies such as field rats, buffalo meat, vegetables and plants from the land.

Isaan is also famous for the production of Thai patterned silks. Silkworms are seen in most villages, being reared by hand in small, home-made, tent-like canvassed bamboo huts, before being woven into the most beautiful and brightly coloured fabric for the rich and famous in Bangkok.

Scenes from Isaan life: Facing page top: a water buffalo market; below: cows on a country road. This page above: 'fishing' in a drained paddy field; below: a marked water buffalo for sale

Surin

Surin is associated, in almost everyone's minds, with elephants – elephants playing football, elephants jousting, or elephants in a tug-of-war contest. This is largely thanks to the Tourism Authority of Thailand (TAT) which, in 1960, decided to host the first elephant round-up festival. So popular was the event that the two-day festival, held in the third week of November, has become an annual feature.

Apart from that time, there are still good reasons to visit the town, which is a picturesque provincial capital and typically Isaan. Trips to Khao Phra Viharn, the great 11th-century ruined Khmer temple situated over the border in Cambodia, can now be arranged through travel agents in Surin, although you should check first with the tourist authority in Bangkok (*tel: 0 2694 1222*). The one thing not to be missed in Surin is the morning market in the centre of the town, where you can eat *larb kwai* (spicy minced water-buffalo meat), and other inexpensive culinary delicacies made by a people renowned for their love of chillies. Here you can sit for hours simply absorbing the provincial feel, the dust, the heat and the raw nerve of Isaan. When it is time to go, just point at your plate, smile, and they will bring a bill.

Surin lies 457km (284 miles) northeast of Bangkok. Trains leave Hualamphong railway station 9 times daily, taking 7 hours. Buses run from the Northern Bus Terminal on Kampaengphet 2 Rd several times daily. If coming during the elephant festival, make sure to have a hotel reservation well in advance.

Imitation Bronze Age pottery from Ban Chiang

Hin Ban Pluang

Near Prasat, 38km (23$^{1}/_{2}$ miles) to the south of Surin, is the 11th-century temple of Hin Ban Pluang, built to honour the Hindu god Vishnu. It is smaller and not as beautiful as the other Khmer-style temples in Thailand, but is certainly worth a visit for those who do not have the opportunity to see these other masterpieces.

Hin Ban Pluang is signposted 5km (3 miles) from Prasat and is best reached by tour or private transport.

Silk Village

The silk village of **Ban Khwao Sinarin**, with its wealth of handwoven products and bracelets, lies 13km (8 miles) north of Surin. Afterwards, continue north to visit the village of **Taklang**, home of the Suay people, where a few elephants are trained throughout the year.

Taklang lies 58km (36 miles) north of Surin near the town of Ban Nong Tat.

Udon Thani

From the airbase at Udon Thani, the US Air Force once dropped bombs on the North Vietnamese, and the city still has some nightclubs and Karaoke bars in its town centre. Visitors now come here to see Ban Chiang, the nearby village which is the site of one of the oldest civilisations in the world.

564km (350¹/₂ miles) northeast of Bangkok. Regular trains from Hualamphong station taking 9 hours, and buses which depart from opposite the tourist office.

Ban Chiang

If the evidence is to be believed, the small town of Ban Chiang may well have existed some 5,000 years ago. That evidence comes from pots and stones, green beads and copper bells discovered by villagers during the early part of the 20th century, and later by excavations undertaken by the University of Pennsylvania and the Fine Arts Department of Thailand government. Even more astounding, these pots carry the same thumb-impressed pattern that has been discovered in Iraq and Turkey.

Besides a delightful museum, with labels in English, the small village has open excavation pits containing pots and skulls.

Ban Chiang is situated 50km (31 miles) east of Udon Thani and is reached by the regular bus services. Museum open: daily 9am–4.30pm. Admission charge.

Stocky, yet impressive, the Hin Ban Pluang honours Vishnu, the Hindu god

The Eastern Gulf

PATTAYA

Most people have heard of Pattaya, the sun, sand and sin city. To some, it is the closest Thailand gets to paradise; to others, it is a seedy, red-light district on the beach. One thing no one can deny: there is no other place like it.

Pattaya's bars are what most people come for rather than its beach, which is brown and grubby. Pubs, beer gardens, boxing rings and cocktail lounges dot the resort where Westerners drink with their Thai paramours. On all sides there are crowded boats, hamburger stalls, revving motorbikes, and murky waters.

In all, Pattaya now has more than

Water scooters on the beach at Pattaya

30,000 hotel rooms with hundreds more coming on stream. The town is surrounded by massive new condominiums and housing developments. Not content with swimming and partying, the town has introduced waterparks, elephants, golf, and even bungee jumping. This is a place for those committed to a certain kind of relaxation.

A touch of 'R and R'

Were it not for the Americans and the Vietnam War, the place they called 'Westerly Winds' might have stayed little more than a stretch of uninhabited sand and palms: when the American soldiers left, the Thais decided that the 'rest and recreation' concept was not such a bad idea after all, and soon foreign tourists began to like it as well. Guest houses sprouted up next to hotels and convention centres, condominiums next to bars and brothels. The only thing that did not come into the picture was planning, and Pattaya has paid the price. Many hotels are now suffering water shortages, many of the beaches are short on clean sand, and the whole resort suffers a shortage of guests.

That is not to say that people do not still love Pattaya. Many have been coming here year after year and swear they will continue to do so. Others enjoy the watersports at Jomtien and the islands, or come for the feel of the place – as Western as it is unreal; where pancakes and waffles are more popular than Thai curries, and where dreams come true for a price.

Girls at a bar in Pattaya

When the lights go out

As the centre for the so-called 'Thai Riviera', Pattaya's nightlife has something for every taste, in theory at least. While topless bars and massage parlours predominate, many hotels have respectable piano bars, violinists or cultural shows.

But go-go bars, massage parlours and clubs are Pattaya's blood, its energy. They are to be found all around the town, but especially at the southern end around the area known as Soi Diamond.

Famous shows are another speciality, but a word of caution: the bevy of beautiful girls that you see in the Alcazar Club on Pattaya Road II or the Tiffany Club at the Pattaya Sport Bazaar Building may not be all they seem.

Along with hundreds of others in the resort, they are part of Pattaya's considerable population of transvestites. While these clubs have become internationally renowned, other *ka toey* (transvestites) hanging out in the bars may be less keen to advertise themselves.

Indeed, for the many men or women who leave Pattaya happy, there are always as many who leave walletless or, worse still, carrying HIV, and while Pattaya may seem a dream, reality can have a nasty knack of catching up with you. *Pattaya lies 147km (91 miles) southeast of Bangkok. The town is easily reached by buses that leave every 30 minutes, and take less than 3 hours, from the Eastern Bus Terminal on Sukhumvit Rd opposite Soi 42.*

PATTAYA ENVIRONS

Pattaya was designed with day trips in mind. Nearby sights cover the full range, from golf courses to tourist villages, from elephants to racing cars, and even include a few places to swim.

Motorbikes and jeeps can be hired on a daily basis, while buses and tours cover all the surrounding destinations.

Coral Islands

Pattaya's great lure was once its islands. Many are now expensive, and the water not as clear, but they continue to attract vast crowds of local and foreign visitors. The biggest, and still the most popular, is **Ko Lan**, 45 minutes away by converted trawler, half that time by speedboat. You can explore the waters around the island (although these are now somewhat polluted) and eat the delicious, if expensive, cuisine the restaurants have to offer. Alternatively, charter a boat to **Ko Phai**. It is just 6km (4 miles) further than Ko Lan, has good food, and the trip may be just the thing for clearing a heavy head.

Boats can be rented from near the tourist office on Beach Road. Rates vary, so bargain hard.

Nong Nooch, popular with children ...

Jomtien Beach is a fine place for watersports

Elephant Village

This is a popular place of entertainment for children as well as grown-ups. Elephants demonstrate their strength, skill and obedience before taking a bath in a creek.

Afterwards you can enjoy elephant rides or play with a cheeky baby elephant. Remember to bring a camera. *Off Highway 3 at km 144.5. Shows: 2.30pm daily. Tel: 0 3824 9818. Admission charge.*

Jomtien Beach

Once considered a separate resort, Jomtien Beach has gradually become an extension of Pattaya. This brought the crowds and concrete, but the beach has managed to survive with less pollution. Jomtien is where most of the windsurfing, sailing and watersports facilities are to be found, as well as some of the best deep-sea fishing in the area. Even absolute beginners on a day trip often bring in fine catches of marlin and sometimes barracuda, especially between November and February. Jomtien has fewer bars than Pattaya, fewer restaurants and, for the most part, less of a feel of fun. Buses and minibuses run regularly between the two resorts which are separated by 6km (4 miles) of headland.

Khao Khieo Open Zoo

The open zoo at Khao Khieo is no African safari park, but it does offer the chance to see some of the wildlife for which Thailand was once renowned. The zoo has Asian, African and European mammals, as well as Thailand's most spectacular aviary, the largest in Asia after Singapore. There are several walks to forests and waterfalls, as well as an education centre and museum.

34km (21 miles) north of Pattaya, near Bang Saen. Can be reached by local bus. Tel: 0 3829 8187/8. Admission charge.

Nong Nooch Village

The beautifully presented Nong Nooch village resort was designed with the jaded tourist in mind. Orchid nurseries, cactus gardens, landscaped gardens and arts and crafts centres all paint an idyllic picture of the 'land of smiles'. It is all a bit commercialised but, if you have children, or will not be able to see the real thing, it can make a pleasant day's outing. Shows start at 9.30 and 10.15am, 3 and 3.45pm, and include folk dances, martial arts, cockfighting and an elephant show.

18km (11 miles) south of Pattaya. Tours can be arranged through the resort office. Tel: 0 3842 9321. Accommodation is also available.

Pattaya Park

This is the closest many people get to water the entire time they are in Pattaya. It has water slides and whirlpools for children; a beer garden, bar and restaurant for the adults. To miss the crowds, come early and avoid weekends.

At 345 Jomtien Beach. Tel: 0 3825 1201.

... and adults, for both its 'wildlife' and natural history

Ang Sila

Best known as the prolific producer of pestles and mortars, the small fishing town of Ang Sila also has a pleasant bay where fishing boats come in. After Pattaya, it is a different world. Fishermen fish and workers work, restaurants sell Thai food, and even the bars are just ordinary places for drinking.

If you continue along the coast you will get to a much-vaunted shrine. This marks the spot where Muk, a young Chinese girl, leapt into the sea when her lover married another woman. He was so distraught when he heard the news that he followed suit. Today, the shrine is a popular gathering point for locals who make offerings to the lovelorn duo.
45km (28 miles) north of Pattaya and 5km (3 miles) from Chon Buri.

Bang Saen

Nobody ever tried to make Bang Saen a hit with foreigners. Thais had already claimed the closest beach to the capital. They descend in crowds every weekend to sit on deckchairs, walk on dirty sand, and eat seafood delicacies. There is a vast aquarium in the Scientific Marine Centre on the university campus, a large waterpark called **Ocean World** signposted along the seafront, and a long, slightly grubby stretch of sand backed by palm trees from which to watch the world.
40km (25 miles) from Pattaya. It can also be reached by local buses from Chon Buri.

Chantha Buri

The gem miners may have been the first to discover Chantha Buri, but the charm

Our Lady Cathedral, Chantha Buri

of the old town and the cool mountain air are slowly beginning to attract a growing number of tourists. The town is surrounded by lush green hills and, in the distance, by the fruit fields that have given this area the reputation for being the fruit garden of Thailand.
312km (194 miles) southeast of Bangkok. Can be reached by air-conditioned buses leaving the Eastern Bus Terminal in Sukhumvit Rd 8 times a day. Regular buses and day tours can be organised in Pattaya.

Our Lady Cathedral

The delightful 19th-century Cathedral of the Immaculate Conception is built in the French style. It is frequented by the local Vietnamese, and is the largest Catholic cathedral in Thailand.
On the far bank of the Chan Buri River, opposite the Sri Chan Rd market.

Gems

These days gems are the main reason for the steady stream of visitors to Chantha Buri. Red rubies and star sapphires are sold in small shops beside the market, and along Trok Kachang Road. Inside these dimly lit shops, or sometimes outside in plain daylight, gems are weighed, costed and sold in lots to be exported (or smuggled) around the world.

Some of these gems still come from the mines around Khao Ploi Waan (Gem mountain). Growing numbers are, however, imported from nearby Cambodia, since most of the local mines have now been exhausted.

8km (5 miles) north of the town, and can be visited on a half-day tour.

Other attractions

Chantha Buri has plenty of other attractions. Khao Kitchakut National Park is 28km (17 miles) northeast of town. In Khao Sabap National Park, 14km (9 miles) southeast, are the beautiful Phliu Falls.

Chon Buri

The nearest major town to Bangkok at only 96km (60 miles) away, Chon Buri is a major centre for sugar and tapioca. It has a couple of temples, the most famous being Wat Yai Intharam, in the centre of town, dedicated to the famous King Taksin who spent the night there before returning to Ayutthaya to defeat the Burmese. Chon Buri is also the place where buffalo races are held every year in October. Traditionally, the buffaloes were helped on their way by a blessing from a Buddhist monk and even a drop of alcohol. With increasing professionalism and bigger rewards, it is now only the owners who get the liquid fortification.

Bus from the Eastern Bus Terminal on Sukhumvit Rd.

A temple in Chon Buri

Ko Chang

The latest paradise islands to draw the attention of developers will not be long in joining Ko Samui and Phuket as prime tourist destinations.

Ko Chang and its 51 surrounding islands, are scattered around the turquoise waters at the southeastern end of the Gulf, far enough away to be slightly off the main track, but accessible enough by means of a four- or five-day outing.

Ko Chang is the main island. Beyond this lie **Ko Kradat**, **Ko Mak** and numerous smaller islands, some of which are still untouched, while others are beginning to arouse the interest of tourists.

A few resorts and bungalows already dot the long stretches of white sand on Ko Chang. Inland, much of the island is covered with jungle, wildlife and scenic waterfalls.

Laem Ngop, the departure point for Ko Chang, lies 80km (50 miles) from Chantha Buri. To get there, catch a bus to Trat, and from there a songthaew *to Laem Ngop. Boats depart every hour during the high season. The best beaches are on the west side of the island. All visitors are strongly advised to take precautions against malaria, which is a major problem.*

Ko Samet

Everyone's most popular weekend choice away from Bangkok, Ko Samet is one of Thailand's most beautiful island national parks and a rapidly developing attraction for the whole province.

It lies just a short distance from the mainland, but far enough for a real, magic island feel. Surrounded by

Fishing is the mainstay of Rayong

turquoise seas and fringed with palm trees, one of its biggest commodities is the pure white crystal sand that covers its beaches. Some of it is enjoyed by appreciative sunbathers, but much of it is of such high quality that it is used by local companies to make glass.

Ko Samet is now so popular that getting accommodation at weekends can be almost impossible. Most visitors come for the sea and sand and place little value on luxurious living. They lie around on the sand, play football on the beaches, listen to guitars and Thai rock music, and eat vast amounts of spicy food.

Older and wealthier tourists tend to go to Phuket or Ko Samui, where they can indulge in better food and more stylish accommodation.

6km (4 miles) off the coast from Ban Phe, to which it is connected by boat. Buses to Ban Phe leave regularly from Bangkok's Eastern Bus Terminal opposite Sukhumvit Soi 42. If you miss the last boat, there are always places to stay in Ban Phe.

Rayong

Famous for its fishing boats, its *nam pla* (fermented fish sauce), and its rubber plantations, Rayong is not a place to spend much time, though it does make a pleasant stop on the way down the coast. Worth visiting is the King Taksin shrine at Wat Lum Mahachai Chumphon, which commemorates the early Siamese king, and the statue of Rayong's most famous inhabitant, Sunthorn Phu, one of Thailand's greatest poets, though his work has yet to be translated into English.

102km (63 miles) southeast of Pattaya. Regular buses run from Bangkok's Eastern Bus Terminal on Sukhumvit Rd.

Nam Pla

This smelly product is the most common accompaniment to Thai food. It is made in Rayong from fermented fish, salt and garlic. Of course, you do not have to come all the way here to try it. Go to any restaurant, ask for *nam pla*, and order yourself a large glass of water. If you can get over the initial taste, you may well become addicted and find yourself transporting vast quantities of it home.

Ko Samet is a naturalist's paradise

Southern Thailand

PHUKET

Thailand's most famous beach resort (pronounced 'Pooket'), also known as the 'Pearl of the South' lies off the west coast, surrounded by the waters of the Andaman Sea. It boasts more than 40km (25 miles) of beaches, numerous offshore islands and a national park. Over the last few years, it has also become a haven for the international jetset with its own airport that receives direct flights from all over the world, five-star hotels, spas, nightclubs, restaurants and golf courses.

Some old-timers now complain that the resort is too expensive and too fashionable. While prices certainly have gone up, and much of the backpack element has gone, you certainly do not have to be rich or famous to enjoy Phuket. Variety in the choice of resorts, hotels and bungalows means that there is something for every taste, whether you want a berth in an international yacht marina, or a simple thatched cottage. Indeed, while Phuket is no longer the

private secret of a few, the simple joys of the sea, the sun and the offshore islands remain as they ever were. It is just that they now come with a touch of the exotic, a touch of the commercial, and a touch of the Western.

Local character

'I know of no place with so much potential,' wrote Captain Francis Light, the first man to recognise the riches of Phuket in the early 1770s. Light was referring to the value of the island's vast reserves of tin, and he spared little thought for its other commodities of sea and sand. Since then, however, the world has discovered Phuket, and Phuket the world.

Phuket may no longer be the deserted hideaway of yesteryear, but it has some of the most varied terrain and the finest seas, not just in Thailand, but anywhere in the world. It also has a strong local character, as anyone who has seen the Vegetarian Festival will testify. The festival takes place during the first nine

The beach at Nai Harn, Phuket, where sunbathing is taken seriously

Phuket

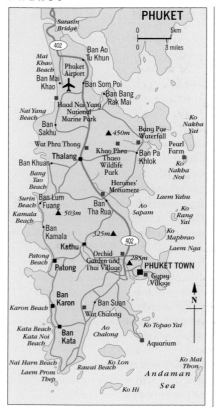

balmy evenings and the abundant supplies of lobster, shellfish and prawns served up in bars and restaurants around the island.

Highlights

One feature that distinguishes Phuket, above all others, is its size. The island covers an area of 540sq km (208sq miles). It is almost as large as Corfu. While, geographically, it is an island, the proximity of the mainland (just 100m/ 328ft away and connected by two bridges) means that there is never a shortage of things to do.

When you have had enough of sun and sea, there is always the Khao Phra Thaeo Wildlife Park, 21km (13 miles) north of Phuket Town, or the grassy promontory of Prom Thep Cape, from where you can watch spectacular sunsets over the Andaman Sea. The beautiful **Phuket Aquarium**, situated 10km (6 miles) from Phuket town on the tip of Panwa Cape, has over 100 varieties of fish to be seen.

Perhaps the greatest highlight, though, is a leisurely exploration of the island by a motorbike or jeep, both of which can be hired locally (*see pp114–15*). Local open-air trucks/buses (*songthaew*) also serve the different resorts, so that those who do not want to risk driving themselves on the steep winding roads can still move freely around.

Thai International operates direct flights to Phuket from Hong Kong, Singapore and Penang, as well as daily flights from Bangkok. These should be booked well in advance. Buses also run from Bangkok's Southern Bus Terminal on Phra Pinklao Rd, taking around 12 hours.

days of the ninth lunar month (usually mid-September), when many of the local Chinese, having abstained from meat for a prescribed period, stick pins through their cheeks and through the skin of their knees, working themselves up into a trance. They then dance on red-hot coals to purify themselves, in accordance with an age-old Chinese belief that remains as pervasive today as ever. At other times of year, the locals prefer a less demanding life: going fishing, sleeping under palm trees like the visitors, or simply enjoying the

Tour: Circuit of Phuket

This tour, by jeep or trail bike, takes you from the historic old town to some of the wildest and most unspoilt beaches on Phuket.

Day trip.

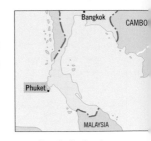

Start in Phuket Town on Ranong Rd. Park along one of the sideroads, and briefly explore the town on foot.

1 Phuket Town

Although it has undergone rapid development, Phuket Town has several beautiful old buildings, witness to the

days when it was a trading hub for the region. Try wandering down Ranong Road. The Thai Airways office is a classic example of the Sino-Portuguese architecture that was fashionable during the late 19th century. Afterwards visit the market on Ranong Road and the Chinese temple of San Jao Jui Tui, scene of the famous annual Vegetarian Festival.
From Phuket town, take route 402, signposted towards the airport. After 13km (8 miles) you will reach the roundabout on which stands the Heroines' Monument.

2 Heroines' Monument

If it were not for these two sisters, Phuket might not be part of Thailand at all. In 1785, Chan and Muk withstood a month-long siege by the Burmese before they went on the attack, dressing up as men and routing the opposition. The grateful islanders have since erected this monument where they make offerings of wooden elephants to the duo.
From the Heroines' Monument continue along route 402 for 6km (4 miles) to Thalang.

3 Thalang

The one-time capital of Phuket, Thalang was besieged, pillaged and destroyed by Burmese invaders in 1809. Little is left of the original town, but there are some charming old wooden houses and a strange Sino-Buddhist temple with *prangs* (spires), dragons and bells.

From Thalang continue on route 402 for 1km (¹/₂ mile) until you see a small turning on the right, signposted to Wat Phra Thong.

4 Wat Phra Thong

Phuket's Temple of the Gold Buddha is home to a famous half-buried Buddha image which was discovered when a young boy tethered his water-buffalo to its topknot (the boy died shortly afterwards). When the Burmese invaded in 1785, they attempted to steal the image, but were attacked by a swarm of angry hornets and driven off. Others who have tried to excavate the statue since have also met with similar unfortunate consequences.

From Wat Phra Thong continue along route 402 for 5km (3 miles), then turn left down route 4031. After 6km (4 miles) turn left down a steep road for Nai Thon.

5 Nai Thon

Here you will find vestiges of old Phuket, with its beautiful coastline, inland rice paddies and water buffaloes, still relatively unscathed by the nearby building spree. Along the coast is a long beach fringed by casuarina trees.

From Nai Thon, continue along the road, past the secluded Bang Tao Beach. The road is steep and subject to erosion, but offers

spectacular views. At Choeng Thale, turn right and follow the signposts for 9km (5¹/₂ miles) to Surin Beach.

6 Surin Beach

This is one of the more peaceful stretches of the island, surrounded by pretty coves but haunted by dangerous currents. The area borders a Thai Muslim village with a flavour quite different from the rest of the island. Wander down the shore and have a snack at one of the beach stalls selling delicious *somtam* (green papaya and garlic) and fish-head curry.

From Surin Beach, continue along the coastal strip, past a beautiful little rock-dominated beach, and from there to Ban Kamala with its lovely stretch of sand. The road climbs steeply before descending at Patong Beach.

7 Patong Beach

The most garish and fun-loving face of Phuket, the 4-km (2-mile) long crescent of Patong gained early popularity among sailors as a dry-season port. Now it attracts not only the US Navy, but every other lover of watersports and entertainment, with its jetskiing, hotels and clubs.

From Patong take route 4029, then turn on to route 4020 which will take you back to Phuket town. Alternatively, take the longer, more scenic route via Karon/Kata, Prom Thep Cape, Rawai and Chalong.

Sisters Chan and Muk led an 18th-century battle that preserved Phuket's independence

Phuket's beaches

Travellers come halfway round the world to visit Phuket because the island offers some of the world's finest beaches. These are mainly located on the sandy, palm-lined west coast, separated by coves and hills. Most visitors, once they have settled in, rarely move. The temptations of sun and sea are too much. But each beach has its own character, so, like choosing a holiday, it pays to shop around and to opt for something that will suit both your pocket and your disposition.

Sparkling beaches lace the coastline

Patong

Rising up from the western coast, the sprinkling of bungalows rapidly gives way to towers, shopping arcades, rows of beer bars, hotels and discos. Big, loud and international, Patong has rapidly overtaken the other resorts to become the king of nightlife and glitzy entertainment. That does not, however, overshadow its other qualities. Patong also has some of the best and whitest beaches with non-stop watersports: parasailing, jet skis, speedboats and windsurfing. One thing Patong is not renowned for is quiet, so if that is what you are after, somewhere further down the coast may prove a safer bet.
15km (9 miles) west of Phuket town.

Karon/Kata

Quiet, calm, and exclusive, the long curving stretch of Karon Beach, situated halfway down the western coast, has rapidly developed into an up-market, but largely family-oriented, area with a string of five-star hotels with swimming pools and garden terraces. Inland, there are still plenty of bars, restaurants and discos, but they are less imposing and less noisy than those of Patong.

Just around the headland is Kata, a smaller stretch of beautiful white sand divided into two parts, with a number of smart hotels and restaurants, but also many cheaper establishments and bars.
16km (10 miles) southwest of Phuket town.

Surin/Pansea

The connoisseur's choice, away from the hustle and bustle. People who come to Surin/Pansea almost inevitably stay in one of the exclusive hotels hidden by palm trees, overlooking the shores. Do not expect lines of nightclubs, though. Surin may have come a long way in the last few years, but it still remains pretty much in its own world, largely cut off from the other beaches by poor roads and still a fair distance from Phuket town. The quality of swimming in Surin does not, however, rank with the other resorts, and the currents can be dangerous.
24km (15 miles) northwest of Phuket town.

Smaller beaches

To the north of Patong are the smaller and quieter beaches of **Kamala Bay** and **Laem Sing**. A few exclusive hotels dot the area which also has the Phuket Fantasea cultural theme park. So far, however, this stretch of land is the closest to Phuket as it was in the old days, with children playing undisturbed on the beaches, and only the odd speedboat breaking the silence. Beware water conditions, however. During the monsoon season, the weather creates vicious undercurrents and can make swimming unsafe. Always check with the locals before you go into the water, as it can be deceptive.

Uncrowded hideaways

Once hideaways were everywhere; now they are a dying breed. But there are some quieter spots around the island, generally not far from the big resorts. For real calm, try the secluded half-moon beach of **Nai Yang**, to the northwest, which has been set aside as a national park and where, at low tide, you can walk for long distances along a relatively deserted coastline.

Uncrowded too is the long stretch of **Mai Khao Beach** that lies further north, and where, between October and February, giant sea turtles come to lay their eggs, and where palms give way to pine trees and picnic spots.

Paragliding is a popular sport in Phuket

A massive limestone outcrop dwarfs Ko Tapu

PHUKET ENVIRONS

The beaches may be Phuket's main attractions, but there is no shortage of sights that can be easily reached as part of a day trip. Almost every big hotel will organise tours. Alternatively, go to any of the local travel agents.

Nakha Noi Pearl Farm

Nakha Noi Pearl Farm is one of the world's largest and best-known cultured-pearl farms. Like others in the vicinity, Nakha Noi is run by the Japanese, who seed oysters to produce the dazzling small stones that are exported to markets around the world.

A few years ago, the farm managed to produce the world's largest cultured pearl, a monster 40mm ($1^1/_2$in) in diameter that weighed just over 30g (1oz). These days, you may not come across pearls of that size, but at Nakha Noi Farm, and at several other farms within the province, you can still see how they are cultured.

Nakha Pearl Tour and Resort, off the eastern coast in Po Bay, 22km

($13^1/_2$ miles) north of Phuket town. Tel: 0 7621 9870. Shows: daily 11am. Admission charge.

Phang Nga

If it wasn't for the James Bond film *The Man with the Golden Gun,* Phuket's top tourist destination might have remained comparatively unknown. Ever since they were featured in the film, the weird and wonderful limestone formations that rise up sheer out of the sea have succeeded in captivating the world, and bring in thousands of tourists every day.

Many lie far out to sea where they house secret caves and can only be reached by using special inflatable rafts. Daily tours will, however, take you by boat to see **Ko Tapu** (Nail Island), with its impossibly sheer rock stack climbing out from the water. Most trips also include a visit to Ko Panyi, a Muslim fishing village on stilts, which has swapped fishing for tourism. Lunch of prawns and lobster here is likely to prove the treat of the day. En route you will be shown a cliff known as Khao Khian (Writing Hill), covered in paintings thousands of years old, which may well be some of the earliest of Thailand's prehistoric remains.

At one point you must pass through a rock tunnel. This is a favourite spot for photographers, who try to frame the picture with a small fishing boat passing through. At other times you will catch views of enchanting outcrops dotted around the sea.

For the more adventurous, sea canoe trips can be arranged to view cave interiors, or to travel to more distant islands where the magic of Phang Nga remains as yet largely unexplored. *87km (54 miles) to the northeast of Phuket. Regular buses leave the Phuket Bus Terminal taking 2 hours (tel: 0 7621 1480). Most people opt for full-day tours.*

Similan Islands

The nine Similan Islands are renowned among diving enthusiasts. They offer some of the most spectacular underwater sightseeing in the Andaman Sea. Wisely, the authorities have seen fit to turn the area into a national park where nature remains relatively at peace, and where the corals and colourful marine life are left more or less intact.

It is best to come anytime from December to May when the waters are at their clearest and the skies are normally a cloudless blue. Part of the islands' appeal lies in their relative solitude. Visitors are mostly day trippers who are gone by the time night falls. For those staying longer, bungalows and camping are available on Ko Similan. Boats can be hired to the other main islands of Ko Ba Ngu and Ko Miang and, these days, often to Ko Born, Ko Payu and Ko Payang.

Off the western coast of Thailand. Can be reached from Phuket in 8 hours by regular boat, or in 3½ hours as part of Songserm Travel's fast day trip (tel: 0 7621 9391, www.seatran.co.th). Between May and November the islands may be inaccessible because of the monsoon.

Cave entrance at Phang Nga Bay

Fast-growing Hat Yai contains a vast number of different shops

TOWNS OF THE SOUTH
Hat Yai

Hat Yai, southern Thailand's largest city, has not grown to what it is as the result of history, nor, for that matter, for its beauty, but because of two equally marketable commodities: its proximity to Malaysia (50km/31 miles away) and its laissez-faire attitude. These have made it the entertainment centre for Malaysian men and a booming centre for smuggled goods.

As a consequence, it has also become the fastest-growing city in the south, far outpacing neighbouring Songkhla to become a sex and sin metropolis par excellence. Down almost every street you will come across a palatial-looking massage parlour, or bars where girls dressed in purple skirts and high-heeled shoes sing love songs until the early hours of the morning.

For non-Malay visitors, Hat Yai has entertainment of a different kind, notably shopping, restaurants and markets.

933km (580 miles) south of Bangkok. Trains leave Bangkok's Hualamphong station several times daily, taking 19 hours. Buses leave from the Southern Bus Terminal on Boromratchonnani Rd. Thai Airways International also has daily flights.

Bullfighting

Once a month, Hat Yai hosts another celebrated spectacle, the bullfight. Do not expect matadors and red cloaks, though. Bullfights here are of a less dramatic quality than in Spain. The bulls fight each other rather than facing a human combatant. Two beasts are brought face to face and left to their own devices. Often the bulls do not move for hours on end, giving time for new bets to be placed. Then all of a sudden, one lowers its head and charges, or the two animals lock horns and push against each other. A victor is declared when one bull runs away or gives ground.

Bullfighting is held at the Klong Wa stadium near the city bus terminal off Rajyindee Rd.

Shopping

Hat Yai's best shopping is to be found off Niphat Uthit 2 and 3 roads where you will find cheap electronic goods smuggled over the border, fake designer T-shirts and handbags. For something different, try the vendors around the Mitrama Hotel on Channiwet Road. They sell the hottest cocktail in town: snake's blood mixed with alcohol.

Another Hat Yai speciality to look out for is doves kept in beautifully carved cages. The birds compete in the local cooing contests, with considerable money awarded to the winners.

Songkhla

A gentle 30-minute bus ride from the busy streets of Hat Yai brings you to Songkhla, the older, more respectable and calmer sister. Songkhla has history and beaches, a delightful fishing port, and the air of a long-forgotten place. You do not see masseuses and coachloads of Malaysians, but you do see people coming to enjoy fresh seafood, piles of prawns and picnics on the sand.
Buses run from Hat Yai to Songkhla every 30 minutes until early evening.

Beaches

Beaches may not be Songkhla's main attraction, but they are popular with the locals. Samila stretches for some 5km (3 miles) along a fairly ordinary stretch of water backed by casuarina trees. Crowds are not a problem, but the sea can be rough.
Samila Beach lies 3km (2 miles) northeast of the town centre. Offshore are the rocky islands known as the 'Cat and Mouse'.

National Museum

Songkhla's former Governor's Palace is a museum piece in its own right. The 1870s building, a delightful example of Sino-Portuguese architecture, houses a good collection of Srivijayan art, as well as items belonging to former governors.
Off Wichianchan Rd. Open: Wed–Sun 9am–4pm. Closed: on public holidays. Admission charge.

Other attractions

Mount Tangkuan, with its *chedis* (pagodas) and its fine views of the inland sea, is worth the climb. Visit the charming old Sino-Portuguese shop-houses on Nakhon Nok and Nakhon Nai Streets. Songkhla will never set the world alight, but it will set the soul at peace.
Hat Yai and neighbouring Songkhla lie south of Bangkok, near the Malaysian border. Nearby sights are the bird sanctuary of Thale Noi at Phattalung, 90km (56 miles) north, and the Khu Khut Waterbird Sanctuary, 40km (25 miles) northeast, near the town of Sathing Phra.

Painted fishing boat, Songkhla

Hua Hin

A quarter of the way down the coast, on the way to the more exotic destinations of Ko Samui and Phuket, is the seaside resort of Hua Hin, known as the 'Royal Resort'.

Prince Chakrabongsae and King Rama VII were two of its earliest admirers. They came here to escape the heat of the capital and prompted the Siamese gentry to follow suit. These days, however, you are more likely to run into modern concrete hotels and condominiums than palaces and aristocracy, although the royal family still come to the palace in Hua Hin for a vacation.

If you are not expecting palm trees and palaces, Hua Hin still exerts its charm. Its beach was made to potter around on, the blue and red deckchairs to sunbathe on, and the cluster of old ladies offer a good traditional, old-fashioned massage.

For a glimpse of the old way of life, wander down towards the pier, which is reached by walking through the old part of town. Take a seat in one of the waterfront restaurants along Naretdamn Road and enjoy some of the wonderful seafood. Nobody will take much notice of you. Only at weekends is the beach crowded with locals escaping from Bangkok.

In the evening, Hua Hin sheds some of its respectability; then the beer bars and outdoor markets come alive, but never to the extent of Pattaya, the sex and sin centre which nestles almost directly opposite on the Gulf of Thailand.

Buses leave approximately every 45 minutes from Bangkok's Southern Bus Terminal on Boromratchonnani Rd. By train from Bangkok's Hualamphong station takes 4 hours. The train stops at the little gem of a station which is itself a monument to Hua Hin's past.

Cha-am

Hua Hin's little sister was, until a few years ago, largely eclipsed. These days the locals have taken a liking to it, although foreigners still prefer the older sister's charm.

Cha-am's sandy beach is long and wide and offers the delights of seafood and paddling. Around the back you will find a small fishing port where you can

Horse riding is an exciting pastime across the beach at Hua Hin

THE OLD RAILWAY HOTEL

No other building, save perhaps for the royal residence of Klai Kangwon ('Far from Worries') has become such a hallmark of Hua Hin as the establishment formerly known as the Old Railway Hotel. For years this was the preserve of the gentry and, during the 1970s, it served as the location for the film *The Killing Fields*. Under the management of the French Sofitel group, the hotel still remains the pre-eminent hotel in Hua Hin.

sit on the rocks and watch the fishing boats steaming out to sea.

There is no need to stay here, though. Hotels in Hua Hin are better. Even so, for a short trip on the regular bus, it makes a nice break and is a good way to see something of the countryside.
25km (15¹/₂ miles) to the north of Hua Hin.

Chopstick Hill

At the southern end of Hua Hin beach is the huge Buddha of Chopstick Hill. If you continue 8km (5 miles) further south, you will reach the protected bay of Khao Tao, once very peaceful, but now being developed.
6km (4 miles) south of Hua Hin. Songthaews run regularly.

Sam Roi Yod National Park

For a pleasant afternoon's trip, visit the lovely Sam Roi Yod National Park, famed among ornithologists for its marsh birds and waders. King Rama IV came here in 1868 to witness an eclipse of the sun, although he died of malaria shortly afterwards. Around the park are beautiful caves, and boats can be hired.
35km (22 miles) south of Hua Hin. To reach it you will need private transport, though you could also join a tour.

Hua Hin lies 220km (137 miles) south of Bangkok. Nearby sights are Cha-am, 25km (15¹/₂ miles) north, the historic town of Phetcha Buri, 66km (41 miles) north, and the beaches of Prachuap Khiri Khan, 90km (56 miles) south.

Rocky drama at Sam Roi Yod National Park

The people of Thailand have a very high regard for their royal family. No single figure contributes so much to the well-being of the people as their king: His Majesty King Bhumiphol Adulyadej Chakri, ninth in the line of the Chakri dynasty.

Born on 5 December 1927 in Cambridge, Massachusetts, Prince Bhumiphol was made king upon the untimely death of his brother in 1946. Over his long reign, he has won the hearts of his people to become the most beloved and most respected of the Chakri monarchs. Seen dressed in finery, or carried down the Chao Phraya on a royal barge, he is the very essence of royalty, a Siamese monarch of old.

His Majesty King Bhumiphol is, however, an extremely progressive and enlightened monarch. Together with his wife, Her Majesty Queen Sirikit, he leads a very active public life. The royal couple can often be seen personally supervising their many projects, including experiments with new agricultural methods and pioneering irrigation schemes, which, in Thailand's agriculture-based economy have a far-reaching impact. In addition, the Silk Weaving Project established under the patronage of Her Majesty the Queen, provides rural families with additional income.

Every December, on his birthday, His Majesty the King of Thailand takes the salute of the nation. Every day, at 8am and 6pm, the national anthem is broadcast over radio and television, and played at public places all over Thailand. Pictures of the king and queen can be seen displayed in prominent places. But more expressive is his presence in the homes of his subjects where, more often than not, his picture can be seen occupying a place of honour. He is rarely forgotten. Thailand has no other comparable figure.

Glimpses of a royal life: Above: King Bhumiphol Adulyadej, Rama IX. Facing page above: King Bhumiphol and Queen Sirikit giving alms to the Buddhist *sangha*; below left: the King ordained as a monk when he was young; below right: the King at Wat Benchamabophit

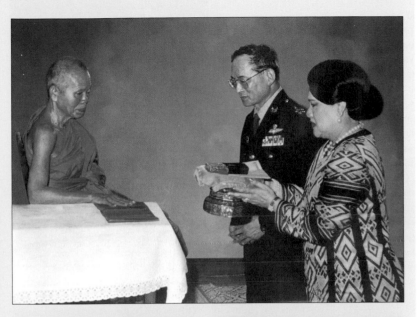

Ko Samui

The word *ko* means island, and Samui must be the archetypal one at that. The two words have become well known among beach lovers around the world. But where once it was only the backpackers who knew them, now Ko Samui is increasingly prized among up-market tourists who fly in for weekends from Bangkok or further afield, to the island's small airstrip.

Gone are the many signs advertising magic mushrooms and the sense of a small community on the edge of a breakthrough. Many former plot owners are now millionaires, while others are involved with the development of bars and discotheques.

Even so, Ko Samui, with its palms and white sandy beaches, has preserved the feel of a tropical island. Here you can still sit in peace and solitude to watch the sunset from the balcony of a simple bungalow. Even the development of new four- and five-star hotels, the thriving discos and restaurants have failed to wrest that completely away.

Coconut territory

If Phuket's coastline is broken up by coves and bays, Ko Samui has one continuous beach running for almost its entire length, while the inland coconut palms have made it one of the biggest exporters of coconuts in Thailand.

That suits every taste, for while Phuket is about activity, watersports, and entertainment, Ko Samui is about relaxation, and only the motorbikes and the tarmac strip around the island hint at the growing inroads made by the modern world.

It takes a monkey four to five days to learn to spin a coconut off its stem

Most visitors explore no further than the Hin Lat waterfall, signposted 2km (1 mile) south of Na Thon, or the strange 'Grandfather' and 'Grandmother' rock formations at the end of Lamai Beach.

Others catch glimpses of the famous pig-tailed macaque monkeys, fervent workers who have put men out of jobs since they have been trained to pick up to 1,000 coconuts a day. Otherwise, you will not find much to do, save to eat a seafood (or Western) lunch, sunbathe in a hammock, or take a windsurfing board out on the water.

Occasionally, even Ko Samui bursts into life when there is a bullfight, but these do not last long, and soon the locals drift back to their coconuts, the foreigners to their sand, their videos, restaurants and discos.

Beaches

Everyone on Ko Samui has a favourite beach, though the speed with which things have developed means that the choice is increasingly segmented into different price ranges. **Chaweng** is still the most popular. The main strip, and home to many of the smart hotels, lies on the east coast, reached by a long climbing road. The smart developments lie at one end, set among palm trees and exotic gardens, but there is still plenty available for those with humbler requirements.

Lamai is a curving bay further to the south. Smaller, humbler, broken up by rocks and coves, it is still more for the budget traveller, although new hotels have made their appearance. Hundreds of huts dot the seafront, but the curving beach dispels any sense of overcrowding. For the evening, numerous discos and restaurants have sprung up behind the beach.

Choeng Mon, not as well known and more exclusive, is set along a beautiful small bay at the northern tip of the island. It is home to several large hotels, and to a beach lined with coconut palms and casuarina trees.

Big Buddha Beach, further to the west, is less popular, but has fine views of two offshore islands. It is beautiful during the summer but choppy during the monsoons, with conditions that may not be suitable for swimming.

All these beaches can be reached by *songthaews* which circulate from the main town of Na Thon until 6pm. Motorbikes and jeeps can also be hired, although care should be taken. *Bangkok Airways flies several times daily from Bangkok to Ko Samui, Phuket, Singapore and Utapao. Alternatively, take the daily train from Bangkok's Hualamphong station to Surat Thani (see p129), a journey of 12 hours. From Surat Thani, a speedboat leaves 3 times a day, taking 2 hours to reach Na Thon on Ko Samui. You are advised to buy a combined rail/ferry ticket that includes transfer.*

Ko Samui lies 80km (50 miles) offshore from Surat Thani. Nearby mainland sights are the historical towns of Nakhon Si Thammarat, 134km (83 miles) to the south, and Chaiya, 40km (25 miles) west.

Ko Samui – a tropical paradise

Around Ko Samui

Once on Ko Samui, you are assured of variety. The island is surrounded by some 80 smaller islands, of which the best known are Ko Phangan and Ko Tao, as well as the beautiful Ang Thong Marine National Park. These can be seen either as part of an organised tour or by regular boats from Ko Samui.

Ang Thong Marine Park

Names like 'Sleeping Cow Island' (Ko Wua Talap), 'Tripod Island' (Ko Sam Sao) and 'Kicking Cow Island' (Ko Wuate) give visitors an idea of what to expect from the Ang Thong Marine Park which lies 29km (18 miles) to the northwest of Ko Samui. For the strange-shaped islands of this archipelago are like gems of rock that have dropped from the sky and congealed in every shape, size and form.

Beautiful caves and waterfalls can be reached along signposted trails that cut through forest and limestone. 'Sleeping Cow Island' is the most popular, offering fine views, bungalows and a campsite. Alternatively, try 'Mother Island' (Ko Mae Ko) with its crystal-clear saltwater lagoon.

Daily boat trips to Ang Thong Marine Park are organised by most tour agents on Ko Samui, leaving Na Thon at 8.30am and returning at 5pm. If desired longer stays can be arranged. Contact Ang Thong National Park (tel: 0 7728 6025) in advance.

Ko Phangan

Ko Phangan, the undeveloped sister island, is just an hour's hop north of Ko Samui by boat, but in terms of scenery and facilities it is like moving to another world. Rough roads circle the island. A better alternative for those wishing to avoid the jolting is to take a boat, either to the southeastern tip of Haad Rin or to the northwest coast around Mae Haad Bay.

On the island, you will find white beaches dotted with palm trees, small bungalows and resorts where the talk among backpackers is of discovering the next beach paradise, and where immediate concerns go no further than the next meal. Offshore, there are opportunities to go snorkelling. Several bungalows now offer flippers and face masks.

Those who appreciate luxury can now visit Ko Phangan for the day. Boats leave Bo Phut Beach on Ko Samui in the morning, arriving at Hat Rin 50 minutes later. There is then just enough time to take a swim and a seafood lunch before catching the return boat to Ko Samui in the afternoon. There are plenty of tours.

Ko Tao

Those in search of greater isolation can also visit Ko Tao, the island that lies three hours north of Ko Phangan and where people spend weeks on end living in small bungalows, eating prawns and coconuts, playing at being a modern-day Robinson Crusoe on the pristine beaches and coral reefs.

A gold Buddha from Nakhon Si Thammarat

Wat Mahathat in Nakhon Si Thammarat

Boats leave irregularly to Ko Tao from Thong Sala pier on Ko Phangan.

Surat Thani

Surat Thani is the mainland jumping-off point for Ko Samui and the islands of Ko Phangan and Ko Tao rather than a destination in its own right. The busy market and a host of foodstalls do, however, offer some consolation if you are waiting for a boat, while several hotels and guest houses provide a resting spot for those who have missed it.

Other attractions

Those with an interest in culture and history may prefer to head north for 50km (31 miles) to the historical town of **Chaiya**. If archaeologists are right, this may once have been the capital of the Srivijaya Kingdom, one of the oldest and most powerful in Asia.

Others may prefer the town of **Nakhon Si Thammarat**, 134km (83 miles) to the south, with its history and its nearby beaches. Both are reached by bus or train from Surat Thani.

Trains leave Bangkok's Hualamphong station daily for Surat Thani, taking 12 hours. VIP runs air-conditioned coaches from Bangkok. Thai Airways also operates daily flights to Surat Thani (www.thaiairways.com).

Krabi

The finest gems in Thailand's beach crown can be described in just one word: Krabi – a world of limestone cliffs fringed by long white beaches that lies a couple of hours east of Ko Phi Phi and a three-hour road (or boat) trip from Phuket.

Ao Nang is the most accessible of Krabi's beaches, and has a booming resort industry. It can be reached by a 25-minute boat trip from Krabi pier or a spectacular road trip through the cliffs.

Ao Phranang is reached only by boat from either Krabi Pier or Ao Nang beach. But it is far more beautiful, with a curving bay, an offshore island and impressive views from Princess Cave. Accommodation, however, is basic and at peak season it can be crowded. *170km (105¹/2 miles) from Phuket by road. Buses leave Phuket two or three times daily from the terminal on Phangnga Road. Songserm Travel also operates buses from Bangkok.*

The Phi Phi Islands

Made famous by the film *The Beach*, these are the most beautiful islands in the world – so say many of the sun-tanned foreigners who have travelled the world looking for idyllic hideaways.

Phi Phi Don and Phi Phi Le are two gems surrounded by palm trees with dreamy bays, spectacular limestone cliffs and long sandy beaches. While Phuket has luxury and Ko Samui an international airport, many parts of Phi Phi have yet to be electrified. The islands do get many tourists, though, and at certain times it can be difficult finding accommodation.

A look-out point on Phi Phi Island

Boats run 5 times a day from Patong Beach on Phuket, taking 2 to 3 hours. From Krabi they run 3 times daily, taking around 2 hours. Trips run in the monsoon season and are only cancelled if a storm is imminent.

Bird's nest soup

Foreigners were not the first people to recognise Phi Phi's potential. The Chinese got here years ago but, rather than opting for a beach holiday, they found a more lucrative resource: the raw ingredients for bird's nest soup. These tiny swiftlets' nests, made up of bird spittle and long renowned for their revitalising quality, can only be reached by climbing bamboo ladders high up in the mouths of the local caves. It is worth it though, for the nests fetch a very high price in the open market.

You can see where the nests come from by visiting **Viking Cave** on Phi Phi Le. Visitors are only allowed at certain times of year so as not to disturb the mating swallows. At other times, you must content yourself with the island's other attractions – boat trips, lazing under palm trees, and eating coconuts and fresh seafood.

Around the islands

Phi Phi Le has no accommodation, although a steady stream of visitors takes advantage of the numerous boats that cross over daily to visit Viking Cave and the beautiful **Maya Bay**. Here you can snorkel and picnic. Further around the bay, there is another chance to explore the corals, then it's back through the turquoise seas to Phi Phi Don in time to watch the sunset.

Experienced divers are spoilt by even greater choice. Underwater coral has made the Phi Phi Islands renowned and, despite damage to the reef caused by the rapid influx of admirers, there is still plenty to see.

Diving trips can be booked, along with deep-sea fishing trips and day tours of the islands, from any of the agents near the pier.

The Phi Phi Islands nestle 2 hours off-shore from mainland Krabi, and are within easy reach of Phuket, Ko Lanta and Ko Hai.

Ao Phranang beach – some people's idea of paradise, though Krabi is developing very fast

Tarutao

Nearing the end of the long, trunk-like isthmus of Thailand, offshore from the town of Ban Pak Bara, lie the 51 islands that make up the **Tarutao Marine National Park.**

Unvisited until recently, the islands remain off the beaten track, and are still difficult to get to. In the 1980s, they were declared a national park, and are now closely monitored by officials trying to preserve the environment. So far, development on the islands has been minimal. Visitors usually rough it out in dormitories, and have to be very lucky to get a bungalow or a tent.

During World War II, Tarutao, the largest of the 51 islands in the national park, was a penal colony. Now visitors come for the beaches with their famous powdery white sand, the islands' inland waterfalls and caves. Diving is one of the great pleasures and boats can be hired to explore the surroundings. Within reasonable distance are the lesser known sister islands of Adang, Rawi and Lipe.

Buses leave fairly regularly from Bangkok's Southern Bus Terminal to Trang (taking around 13 hours). From there you must catch a songthaew *to the small fishing village of Ban Pak Bara. Boats to Tarutao leave from here twice daily in season.*

TOWNS OF THE DEEP SOUTH
Narathiwat

At Narathiwat, you have almost reached the end of the road as far as Thailand is concerned. Beyond lie the border towns of **Sungai Kolok** and **Ban Taba**.

Few visitors come this far south. Anyone who does will discover a town lazily unaware of its own charms, with its wide, shady streets crossed by tricycles, and its inhabitants dressed in colourful batik.

The locals seem in little hurry to change that, and the only apparent sign of activity is in the markets.

A 6-km (4-mile) *songthaew* ride to the southwest of the town is Wat Khao Kong, with its vast bronze, 25-m (82-ft) high Buddha. At the other end of town is Hat Narathiwat beach, less developed than others elsewhere, and with less exotic appeal, but still good for a paddle (beware the currents) or as a place to enjoy local snacks.

PEOPLE OF THE DEEP SOUTH

More than two million Muslims live in the provinces that make up the far south of Thailand. They are the second biggest minority in the kingdom, a people who have traditionally sided with Malaysia. Most of them are farmers or fishermen living in small communities, although several big towns do exist. In the past, friction with the Thais and calls for a separate homeland have vitiated the situation in the south. These days resentment continues, but a strong military presence, as well as a royal palace, are there to make sure it does not get out of control.

Narathiwat is 1,315km (817 mies) from Bangkok, and can be reached by buses from the Southern Bus Terminal on Boromratchonnani Rd.

Pattani and Yala

Northwest from Narathiwat, and easily reached are Pattani 100km (62 miles) and Yala 100km (67 miles). These towns bear the hallmarks of Islam and the influence of nearby Malaysia. Few tourists come down this way; they are told it is unsafe because of separatist conflicts. Visitors should check with the local police station first. Those who do venture so far will almost inevitably be rewarded with glimpses of unspoilt rural villages and beautiful countryside.

Offering prayers at a Chinese temple

Fishing boats at Pattani

Getting away from it all

Adventure travel in Thailand may have lessened with the opening up of the kingdom and the rapid influx of tourists, but the sheer size of the country and the fact that visitors concentrate on a handful of sights, means that there is always something different near at hand for those with a little more time or a sense of adventure. Most trips can be organised using public transport. These days, there is also no shortage of travel companies offering tours, and the bigger hotels always have something organised.

Abundant marine life around Thailand's coast attracts a variety of birds

Remember two basic rules: do not go off into isolated areas alone; and beware the border areas, especially around the Golden Triangle. Other than that, make the most of the opportunities. Thailand still has some of the most beautiful and undiscovered spots in the world, and people who make the effort to find them will almost certainly be well rewarded.

Birdwatching

Colourful waders, orange-breasted and red-headed trogons, moustached barbets and flashy kingfishers are just some of the birds that can be found in the national parks. They are part of a vast ornithological population estimated to include over 900 species. Some are unique to Thailand. Others migrate from as far afield as northern China and Siberia to escape the cold.

Two of the best spots for the visiting birdwatcher are the **Thale Noi Bird Sanctuary** and the **Khu Khut Waterbird Sanctuary**, both within easy reach of Hat Yai and Songkhla (*see pp120–1*). Trips can be arranged from either town

through tours, or by public transport. **Khao Yai National Park**, situated just a couple of hours northeast of Bangkok, also has one of the biggest populations of hornbills in Southeast Asia. Another good, and more accessible, place to see birds is the highly popular **Khao Khieo Open Zoo** near Pattaya.

Remember to bring binoculars, a book for identification, and a lot of patience; Thailand may still have many birds, but those that are left have grown wise to the ways of the world and are often heard, but rarely seen.

Buddhist meditation

It may not be adventure travel in the physical sense, but Buddhist meditation is rapidly gaining acceptance throughout the Western world, and what better place to try it than in Thailand itself.

Courses can be for anything from one day to two weeks, and range in content from simple meditation to vigorous pursuit of the key precepts. Those who wish to attend meditation classes during their stay in Bangkok can do so at **Wat**

Mahathat (the International Buddhist Meditation Centre). Classes are also held at **Wat Bowonniwet,** and at the **World Fellowship of Buddhists.**

Outside the capital, one of the most popular centres is located at **Suan Mokhapalaram** in Surat Thani province, where a large, tree-filled park provides an ideal ambience for discovering peace of mind. Classes last for 10 days from the first of each month.

Caving

Until someone produced statistics showing that Thailand has one of the biggest caves in the world, no one really bothered about them much, except as a setting for Buddha statues. Now people are beginning to explore them, although a local guide is essential. Probably the best known is **Tham Lot,** situated 9km (5^1/$_2$ miles) from the town of Soppong in Mae Hong Son province (*see p90*); further down the road is another vast

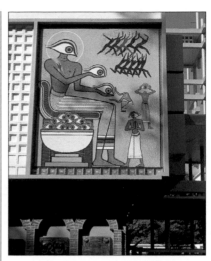

The temple of Wat Suan Mokhapalaram

cave. Guides can be hired at the Cave Lodge Guest House. In the south, caves can be explored on **Ao Phranang** near Krabi (*see p130*), and at **Phang Nga** near Phuket (*see p118*).

Waterbird sanctuary near Songkhla

Climbing

Thailand's highest peak, Doi Inthanon near Chiang Mai, is only 2,565m (8,415ft) high, so there is not much opportunity for alpine sports, or ropes and crampons. The country does, however, have plenty of opportunities for steep hiking. **Khao Yai** (*see p63*), **Loei** (*see p98*) and **Doi Inthanon** (*see p80*) all offer slopes sufficiently steep to test even the fittest. Before attempting them, contact the National Parks Division in Bangkok (*tel: 0 2562 0760*) for details, and enquire about a guide. You are unlikely to find sheer rock faces, but you will find fine views and staggeringly beautiful countryside.

Island hopping

You do not have to go far in Thailand to find a perfect island, but to explore a whole string of them, or to find one uninhabited takes more time and effort.

The best starting off points for island hopping are **Krabi** and **Ko Phi Phi** (*see pp130–1*), and **Phuket** (*see p112*). The best method of exploring them is either by charter (relatively expensive) or by regular public boat services.

From Ko Phi Phi, you can jump on a regular boat which will take you to **Ko Lanta**, and from there to **Ko Hai** and **Ko Muk**. Some people have even managed to work their way all the way down to **Ko Tarutao** in the far south. On the east coast, there are regular boats from Chumphon to **Ko Tao**, and from there to **Ko Phangan** and **Ko Samui**, and vice versa.

New services are springing up all the time but, while they make access to the many other islands a great deal easier,

Powerful tourist boats bring even the remotest islands within reach

they make the discovery of the deserted island more elusive.

Motorbiking

Motorbikes provide one of the best and most popular ways of getting to see the countryside – 125cc, 250cc and even 750cc bikes can be rented by the day in the majority of tourist destinations.

Some of the best motorbiking is to be had in the winding roads and dirt tracks of the north, around Chiang Mai, Mae Sai and the Golden Triangle. From here you can tour around Chiang Rai or follow the road circuit westwards via Pai to Mae Hong Son and Mae Sariang. Roads are generally in reasonable condition, although beware of oncoming trucks and buses, which tend to take up the whole road. Also, never drive at night or by yourself.

Motorbikes generally cost upwards of 300 baht a day, although the big bikes cost correspondingly more. All you really need is a 125cc bike, though preferably a petrol one, rather than a diesel guzzler.

The wearing of helmets is mandatory. Before taking it, check the bike as you will be responsible for any damage sustained on the way. Finally, take care: accidents and injuries are numerous.

National parks

National parks, to anyone who has been to Africa, mean abundant wildlife. Thailand's parks offer sights that are different but as good: natural beauty, flowers and waterfalls, and some of the last unspoilt spots in the country. With as many as 103 national parks scattered throughout the kingdom, there is no

One of the easiest, but by no means the safest way to explore Thailand

lack of choice. Some parks are on the mainland, while others consist of islands. Some are reached by boat, others by jeep or bus.

The most popular and easily accessible from Bangkok is **Khao Yai** (*see p63*), which has one of the largest concentrations of wildlife in the country. In the south are the island parks of **Tarutao** (*see p132*) and the **Similans** (*see p119*). The north and northeast has **Doi Inthanon** (*see p80*) and **Phu Kradung** (*see pp98–9*).

Most national parks offer accommodation, and some even provide meals. If you are planning on spending time there, always make a reservation in advance. If you are thinking of trekking, try to arrange a guide as well as maps, sleeping bags, malaria tablets and a Thai dictionary. For bookings, contact the National Parks Division on Phahon Yothin Road in Bangkok (*tel: 0 2562 0760*).

Elephants, monkeys, tortoises and beautiful birds are all part of nature's gift to the kingdom, and while some of Thailand's vast forests have been cut down, many areas still remain relatively unspoilt havens for wildlife.

The rich forests, countryside, coasts and hills of Thailand are breeding grounds for some of the last true remaining wildlife in Asia. The most common species still found are gibbons, macaque monkey and sambar deer, although even these are dwindling in number. An estimated 200 tigers are also said to live wild in the Myanmar border areas, along with rapidly declining numbers of elephants. The elephant is Thailand's most revered animal, and also its national symbol, once featured on its flag, but that hasn't deterred poachers.

Thailand's forests, flowers and lush tropical vegetation are more easily enjoyed. In the north, there are still large areas of evergreen and teak forest protected as national parks, while the south has vast areas of mangrove. Here too, in Songkhla (see p121), is to be found some of the kingdom's most spectacular birdlife, including kingfishers, warblers and numerous species of waders. Take a long-tailed boat and admire the living quarters of the many birds – lotus flowers! Discovered by locals, the Doi Inthanon National Park in Chiang Mai is also fast becoming a very popular new area for birdwatching.

Near Bangkok is the Keang Krachan Dam and National Park in Phetcha Buri province. Here, visitors can walk along well-marked pathways into a rainforest to see some of the best wildlife Thailand has to offer. Further south, Khao Sak is accessible from Phuket and Phang Nga. The Tourism Authority of Thailand is highlighting Khao Sak as the best destination in southern Thailand for ecotourism. This is the home of some large mammals, as well as the famous hornbill. However, due to lack of awareness, the number of visitors is still small.

Thailand's natural environment has come under increasing pressure, to some extent because of development, but especially with the plunder of wildlife. However, with the support of determined national park officials, implementing the recommendations of independent researchers, it is hoped that further damage to wildlife and nature will be prevented, and that the kingdom's spectacular natural beauty will be preserved for future generations to appreciate.

The Atlas moth, the world's largest moth is found in the forests of Thailand where the gibbon (facing page below) and varieties of orchids (this page) can also be seen

Rafting

Rafting offers one of the most delightful ways of seeing the countryside for those who have the time and are willing to put up with the discomfort.

The rafts are generally made from bamboo tied together with twine, and comprise little more than a roof and floor. During the day they float, or are towed, along the river, while at night they are moored on the river bank. You sleep on board or, better still, stay in local villages.

Rafts can be hired in Kanchana Buri (*see p62*) for a relaxing two days on the Khwae Noi River to Sai Yok National Park. For an even more fascinating trip, in which you get to see both the countryside and the colourful hill tribes, hire a raft from Tha Ton to Chiang Rai (*see pp86–7*), and take a guide with you, who will steer, cook and arrange tours of the villages for the three-day trip.

Because rafts in Tha Ton are made to order, you must request one at least three days before departure.

Sailing

Two coastlines, turquoise seas, and uninhabited islands make Thailand ideal for sailing. Boats for hire now cater to every standard, ranging from old-fashioned schooners to world-class racers, and almost all of them offer the comforts and luxury of a five-star cruise.

Most visitors start out from Phuket or Pattaya. Trips last for anything from one day to two weeks, and can take you as far as the Similan Islands, the Surin Islands, or even to Langkawi and the Malaysian border.

Bamboo raft at Tha Ton in northern Thailand

The best time of the year for sailing depends on the monsoon. During this rainy season you may find that even the legendary turquoise seas will look an unhealthy grey. The Andaman Sea is best from November to May; the Gulf of Thailand season extends from May to October.

Trekking to the tribes

Almost everyone who visits the north will, at some stage, pack their rucksack and walk for anything ranging from a day to a week in search of the minority ethnic peoples known as the hill tribes. Many will enjoy it. Some will hate it.

Trekking in Thailand has become an extremely popular form of adventure travel, involving gentle walks in the countryside, visits to the various hill tribes, and boat trips down the rivers. Some up-market treks include elephant rides and air-conditioned buses.

The primary aim of a trek is to see the tribes, and the best way of doing this is on foot. After spending the night in a village, you will start at dawn, walk perhaps 8km

(5 miles), then stop for lunch before continuing to another village and stopping in the early evening. If you are lucky you may then be able to sit with the tribespeople and, with your guide acting as interpreter, gain an insight into their way of life. If you are unlucky, you will find yourself placed in a separate hut kitted out for foreigners, eating a pot of noodles your guide has provided.

With countless trekking centres in Chiang Mai, Chiang Rai and, increasingly, Mae Hong Son, deciding what sort of trek to choose is no easy matter. Try to check with the tourist authorities, and talk to other trekkers who have returned from a trip.

Finally, before paying up, find out exactly what is included, what kind of transport you will have to take back, and who will be providing the food. Below is a list of some agencies in Chiang Mai. All the big hotels also run their own trekking services.

EastWest Siam Down Town Inn Hotel
Tel: 0 5328 1789; www.ewsiam.com
Libra Trekking
28 Soi 9 Moonmuang Rd.
Tel: 0 5321 0687.
Siam Travel Service
145 Chang Khlan Rd. Tel: 0 5327 2367.
The Trekking Collective Company
25/1 Ratchawithi Rd. Tel: 0 5341 9079;
e-mail: alttreks@cm.ksc.co.th

Kata Beach, Phuket, is an ideal place for sailing

Shopping

From teak-wood elephants to colourful umbrellas, lacquerware bowls and trendy fashionwear, Thailand offers some of the best buys in one of the best places for shopping in the region. Indeed shopping has, in many ways, become the country's latest gift to tourists, with some great bargains on offer.

Folk handicrafts at a fair in northern Thailand

Do not, however, expect to buy cameras, or, for that matter, DVDs. If those are the sort of goods you are after, better to wait for Hong Kong or Singapore. What Thailand does have is exquisite and well-priced handicrafts, silks, gems and clothes. In many parts of the country, especially around Chiang Mai, you can see the goods being made – lacquerware pots being sprayed by hand or lumps of timber being carved into shapely bowls.

Above all, what characterises shopping in Thailand is the sheer joy of it. Whether you are looking for bargains or souvenirs, or simply enjoying a stroll, shopping is fun and provides a fascinating insight into the daily life of the people.

Value for money

Getting value for money is never hard, but squeezing out the last penny can be quite a job. Before asking, work out how much you are prepared to pay, then bargain hard. Never appear over-anxious to buy, always smile and laugh. Bargaining, though it takes time and trouble, can be the most rewarding part of shopping.

To get the very best prices, always consider buying several items from one shop and, if possible, compare prices at one or two. Two shops right next to each other may offer vastly different prices.

Markets are normally the best places to shop at. Shopping centres are usually slightly more expensive, but for those who prefer fixed prices, they may prove a less perilous alternative. Do not dismiss hotel arcades; they generally provide reliable goods at quite reasonable prices.

Lastly, a word on fakes. These can be found in many stalls and shops. Some of them are almost as good as the originals. Often it is a matter of luck how long they last. Some people have worn fake Rolex watches for years without trouble, while others have found that theirs packed up after a week. But with very low prices for items such as big-brand watches, VCDs, CDs and pre-recorded cassettes, you are never going to be too disappointed.

To tell a fake watch, feel the weight. To tell fake jeans, feel how thin the cloth is. To tell other fakes, check the price and use your judgement.

Dos and don'ts

Many shops now have a sign on their window resembling an ancient pair of weighing scales. This means they have the approval of the Tourist Authority of Thailand (TAT). That does not always guarantee original goods, and it certainly will not give you a price-back guarantee, but it does provide one of the best indicators of a reliable retailer.

Ultimately, when listening to a gem or antiques dealer you must trust your own instincts. Behind the smiles and the charm are some very smart traders. Whatever people tell you, you should always be aware that antiques and Buddha images cannot be taken out of the country without official permission which may not always be forthcoming.

Many shops do, however, offer export services so that you can post your lacquerware elephants directly to your home, either by ship or by air.

The TAT provides a shopping booklet with recommendations. If you have complaints, go and speak to them, although in practice there is little they can do.

Most shops are open between 9.30am and 6pm, most markets from dawn, but at almost any time you can be sure of finding something that will be open for a spot of last-minute shopping.

Thai gold jewellery is exquisitely crafted as depicted by these chains on display

What to buy
Antiques

The oldest thing about antiques is the adage 'don't be taken in by them'. Fakes are many and originals few. Even so, you may discover some real collectors' items, including: Ming pottery, Thai and Chinese ivory figures, and fabulous old woodcarvings. The gradual opening up of Indo-China has unleashed a wave of products from Myanmar, Cambodia, Laos, China and Vietnam such as bronze drums, silver figures, carved wood panels and tapestries.

Unless you are an expert, fake or reproduction antiques provide a safer option at much lower prices. Attractive tapestries, old *khon* masks (used in classical Thai dancing) and carved animals are all beautifully designed, and you know what you are getting.

Clothing

In Bangkok, tailors will run up shirts, jackets and skirts in a matter of hours. The quality of workmanship may not, however, be as high as in Singapore or Hong Kong, and it pays to shop around.

To start with, check out different styles and cuts. If you want a tailored suit or dress, make sure you opt for good cloth. Also try to bring an exact copy of what you want, as Thai ideas of fashion and those of Westerners can vary widely.

Boutique wear and designer fashion industries have grown rapidly and become one of Thailand's biggest sources of export income. Bangkok and Chiang Mai are the best places to pick clothing up. In Bangkok, try the big shopping centres in Siam Square or the

Ceramics and Benjarong ware for sale

Peninsula Shopping Centre near the Regent Hotel to get an idea of the immense variety on offer.

Other than that, T-shirts, fake designer jeans and beachwear can be found in abundance almost everywhere, and at prices far lower than back home.

Handicrafts

Beautiful handicrafts are a Thai specialty. They range from colourful quilts to leather wallets and artificial flowers. Lacquerware dishes, made from bamboo, sprayed with layers of varnish, are especially popular, as are rattan baskets, patterned porcelain jars and stylised dolls. Other perfect gifts, such as the famous hand-painted umbrellas, you can actually watch being made along Chiang Mai's San Kamphaeng Road (*see p72*).

In Bangkok, you will find products from all over and, generally speaking, the prices are only marginally higher. What you will not have is the satisfaction of seeing them made.

Jewellery

Thailand offers some of the world's keenest prices for precious and semi-precious stones, but only for the real connoisseurs. For those who do not know the ropes, it can prove an expensive education.

Jade, Burmese rubies, blue or black star sapphires and turquoise are what the experts come for. Silver and gold are also popular, with beautifully made and intricately designed niello-work bracelets inlaid with black alloy.

Often the safest place to buy jewellery is in one of the big hotel boutiques or at a TAT-recommended shop. Never go with a tout, always get a letter of authentication, and remember that, for every person who gets a bargain on gems, there are probably four or five who make a loss on them.

Thai silk

More than any other product, Thailand is associated with silk. The country breeds silkworms, produces yarn, weaves and exports some of the finest silk in the business.

Thai silk is characterised by a coarse texture, with an infinite range of colours and a natural filament that makes the resulting fabric crease-free.

Prices vary enormously between the products of **Jim Thompson's** on Bangkok's Surawong Road, and the smaller boutiques and stalls nearby. As a rule, silk here is marginally cheaper than in Hong Kong, but more expensive than in India.

Most shops will run up tailor-made designs but, as with clothing in general, take care about cut and design and give them as much time as possible.

Thai silk is world famous and readymade dresses perfectly tailored

Where to buy

BANGKOK

Antiques

Anong Gallery
2nd Floor, Peninsula Plaza.
Tel: 0 2252 3070.
Gallerie@444
4/F River City Complex.
Tel: 0 2237 0077 ext. 444.
Silom Galleria
Silom Rd.
Tel: 0 2630 0944.

Gems and semi-precious stones

Blue River Diamond
Peninsula Plaza
Tel: 0 2253 6107.
Gems Gallery
Rama VI Rd.
Tel: 0 2271 0150.

Handicrafts

Bangkok Dolls
Soi Ratchataphan, Ratchadamri Rd.
Tel: 0 2245 3008.
Chitrilada Shop
Oriental Plaza.
Naraiphand
127 Ratchadamri Rd.
Tel: 0 2252 4670.
Rasi Sayam
82 Sukhumvit Soi 33.
Tel: 0 2262 0729.
Tamnan, Amarin Plaza
3rd Floor, Phloen Chit Rd.
Tel: 0 2256 9929.

Metalware displayed in an antique shop

Tailor-made clothes

Classic Style
95 Naret Rd.
Tel: 0 2236 1916.
Perry's
60/2 Silom Rd.
Tel: 0 2233 9236.
T Design
3rd Floor, River City Shopping Complex, Charoen Krung Rd.
Tel: 0 2252 9650.

Thai cotton and silk

Design Thai
304 Silom Rd.
Tel: 0 2235 1553.

Jim Thompson's
9 Surawong Rd.
Tel: 0 2234 4900.
Silk Corner
2nd Floor, River City Shopping Complex, Charoen Krung Rd.
Tel: 0 2237 0077.
Thai Shinawatra
Rama IV Rd.
Tel: 0 2633 1200.

CHIANG MAI

Antiques

Baan Phor Liang Muen's
36 Phrapokklao Rd, Soi 2.
Tel: 0 5327 8187.

Baan Yuttana
131 Ban Thai.
Tel: 0 5344 1570.
Borisoothi Antiques
15/2 San Kamphaeng Rd.
Tel: 0 5333 8460.

Ceramics
Mengrai Kilns
79/2 Arak Rd.
Tel: 0 5327 2063.
Siam Celadon Factory
San Kamphaeng Rd.
Tel: 0 5333 1526.

Handicrafts
Baan Benjawan
Chiang Mai-
San Kamphaeng Rd.
Tel: 0 5333 1546;
www.baanbenjawan.com

Boon Lacquerware
5/2 Mu 6, San
Kamphaeng Rd.
Tel: 0 5333 1407.
Hilltribe Products
Foundation
21/17 Suthep Rd.
Tel: 0 5327 7743.
Night Bazaar
Chang Khlan Rd.
Northern Tribal Crafts
204/2 Bamrung Rat Rd.
Tel: 0 5324 1043;
www.ttcrafts.co.th

Jewellery and
silverware
Gems Gallery
80/1 Chiang Mai-
San Kamphaeng.
Tel: 0 5333 9307.

Lanna Thai
79 San Kamphaeng Rd.
Tel: 0 5333 8015.

Thai silk and cotton
Bua Bhat Phanit
147/4–5, Chang Khlan Rd.
Tel: 0 5327 5741.
The Loom
27/3 Ratchamankha Rd.
Parn Chiang Mai
189/22 Chang Khlan Rd.
Tel: 0 5327 5119.
Piankusol
56 Mu 3, San Kamphaeng
Rd.
Tel: 0 5333 8040.
Shinawatra Thai Silk
145/1–2 San Kamphaeng
Rd.
Tel: 0 5333 8053.

Intricate, brightly coloured and wonderfully life-like Thai dolls are popular with locals and visitors alike

All the colours, sights and sounds of Thailand are to be found in its markets. They are the traditional commercial hub, the source of wholesale goods and, most of all, a demonstration of the Thai vitality and love of life. Fresh produce arrives after an overnight ride

from the provinces, including beautiful flowers still covered in dew, baskets of red and green chillies, hundreds of varieties of banana, pineapple and the strangely scented 'king of fruits', the durian. Live pigs arrive slung over the back of motorbikes, along with pots and pans piled to

bursting point on the back of trucks and *tuk tuks*.

They are joined by tricyclists selling dried squid, locals selling steaming mounds of noodles, beggars, restaurateurs, everyone seemingly with at least some sense of purpose, everything that a photographer hoping to capture the real Thailand could wish for.

Twenty years ago this was the only way to get your produce. Now there are supermarkets and hypermarkets, but for the real connoisseurs or those on a budget, markets are still the only place to come.

It is not difficult to find a market; all you generally need do is wander down any pavement until you run into a collection of stalls. These normally start trading well before dawn and are at their best before the start of the heat and the dust. Local villages live around markets. You will encounter an abundance of weekly or daily markets in the smallest of villages. Locals will usually only sell one or two things on each stall. The ripped plastic canvases linked together with string are usually very low, with only just enough room to move around. Locally produced vegetables, meats, flowers, plus an array of bric-a-brac are the norm. Watch out for flies!

The most famous market of all is based in Bangkok. Started as a small village market on a Sunday, the Chatuchak Market has taken over an area bigger than a football pitch, and is open on Saturdays and Sundays from dawn to dusk. Here you will find everything anyone could possibly want, from a cobra to a potted plant, designer fabrics to car spare parts, antiques to Chinese artefacts. If you are in Bangkok over the weekend, definitely pay a visit. In the south, Hat Yai, on the border with Malaysia, is renowned as another major market city. Here, you will find a huge choice of food, flowers and fantastic fruits, all brought in from Malaysia, and on sale almost 24 hours a day. Everywhere, always beware of pickpockets.

Thai markets come in all shapes and sizes, mostly selling vegetables and fruit, including the extraordinary durian (above)

Entertainment

No other country in Asia rivals Thailand when it comes to night-time entertainment. From its bars and boxing to the quieter spectacles of classical dancing, the country outdoes all its competitors. Whether you are alone or in company, a night owl or an early bird, you will always find something worth staying up for. The best place for nightlife is, of course, Bangkok, but Pattaya, Phuket, Chiang Mai and, increasingly, Ko Samui offer various forms of entertainment, boisterous or otherwise.

Traditional fan dances are still popular

Bars

Missing out on Patpong would be like coming to Athens and not visiting the Parthenon. Bangkok's world-renowned red-light strip is the most popular single tourist site in the city (*see p44*).

For the most part, the emphasis is on innocent fun, with the air more of a party than a brothel. Besides the bars and sex shows there are night markets, piled high with a fantastic array of fake goods, restaurants and food stalls – indeed, everything that a red-light district generally is not.

When you enter a bar, always check the price of a drink, and ask whether there is an entry charge or an entertainment charge. Some upstairs bars are known as 'clip' joints. They will try to charge you an exorbitant price for a drink. If this happens, never struggle or cause a fight. Pay up and immediately report it to the tourist police who are conveniently situated at either end of the road. They will then accompany you back to the bar and you will get your money back.

Some bars provide other surprises. Bangkok has a growing number of transvestites as well as a special strip for gays. But beware the statistics: AIDS remains a problem, and other sexually transmitted diseases are endemic.

Besides Patpong Road, Bangkok has several other red-light districts. Soi Cowboy is situated between Sois 21 and 23 Sukhumvit Road, while the raunchier, and much more down-market Nana Plaza is on Soi 4 Sukhumvit Road.

Cinemas

Cinemas have a prolific concentration both in the capital and throughout the provinces. Most of them are extremely cheap, and Thai films contain every conceivable element of violence and romance, religion and comedy, all in one. These days, however, there are also plenty of cinemas in Bangkok showing English-language films with Thai subtitles. For details of what's showing where, check the local newspaper.

Discotheques and live music

Thailand now has some of the largest discos in the world. For a real eye-opener try Bangkok's Nasa Spacedrome with its 3,000-capacity crowds, and waitresses dressed in space-age uniforms. A number of the big hotels, such as the Dusit Thani and the Shangri-La, also have their own discos which play a mixture of Thai and Western music.

Bangkok also has excellent rock clubs, a host of jazz bars, and occasionally even a string quartet. Details of special performances are given in *The Nation* and *The Bangkok Post*, as well as the free distribution magazines found in almost all hotel foyers.

Pubs and hotel bars

That veritable old institution, the English pub, is not forgotten in Thailand. A range of old-worldly, roast-beef-eating, pint-sinking opportunities

Bangkok stays alive well into the night

are there, although mainly in Bangkok, Pattaya and Phuket.

Finally, if that all sounds too much, try the terrace bar at the Oriental Hotel, an idyllic experience, or the Shangri-La Hotel, or any other of the quiet hotel cocktail bars on Bangkok's Chao Phraya River. You will not be disappointed.

Traditional drummers perform for tourists in a hotel

BANGKOK
Cinemas
Lido Multiplex
Opposite the Siam Centre,
Rama I Rd.
Tel: 0 2252 6498.
Scala
Siam Square, Soi 1.
Tel: 0 2251 2861.
SF Cinema City
Mahboonkrong Centre.
Tel: 0 2260 9333.
Siam
Siam Square.
Tel: 0 2251 3508.

Discos
Concept CM²
Novotel Bangkok, Siam
Square.
Tel: 0 2255 6888.

Nasa
999 Ramkamhaeng Rd.
Tel: 0 2214 3368.

Go-go bars
Goldfinger
66 Patpong 1 Rd
(Ground Floor).
King's Castle
54/56 Patpong 1 Rd
(Ground Floor).
Queen's Castle
100 Patpong 1 Rd.
Safari
Patpong 1 Rd
(Ground Floor).

Live music
Blue Moon
145 Gaysorn Rd,
Ratchaprasong.
Tel/fax: 0 2253 7607.
Brown Sugar
231/20 Sarasin Rd.
Tel: 0 2250 1826.
Saxophone
3/8 Victory Monument,
Phya Thai.
Tel: 0 2246 5472.

Pubs
Bobby's Arms
1st Floor, Carpark,
Patpong 2.
Tel: 0 2233 6828.
Jools
21/3 Soi Nana Tai,
Sukhumvit Rd.
Tel: 0 2252 6413.
The Witch's Tavern
306/1 Soi 55 Sukhumvit.
Tel: 0 2391 9791.

CHIANG MAI
Bars and pubs
Mai Tai Lobby Bar
Novotel Chiang Mai,
Chang Phuak Rd.
Tel: 0 5322 5500.
Opium Den
Up-market cocktail bar.
Chiang Mai Orchid Hotel,
Huai Kaeo Rd.
Tel: 0 5322 2099.
Riverside
Jazz and meals.
9/11 Charoen Rat Rd.
Tel: 0 5324 3239.

Discos
Bubbles Disco
Porn Ping Hotel,
Charoen Prathet Rd.
Tel: 0 5327 0099.
Crystal Cave
Empress Hotel,
Changkhlan Rd.
Tel: 0 5327 0240.
Gigi
Chiang Mai-
Lamphun Rd.
Tel: 0 5330 2401.

Northern dancing
Old Chiang Mai
Cultural Centre
185/3 Wua Lai Rd.
Tel: 0 5327 5097.

PATTAYA
Bars and pubs
Garden Bar and
Piano Bar
Exclusive, with beautiful
views.

Royal Cliff Beach Resort.
Tel: 0 3825 0421.
Green Bottle Pub
Pattaya 2nd Rd.
Tel: 0 3842 9675.
Soi Diamond
Biggest concentration
of beer and 'go-go'
bars.
South Pattaya.

**Cabarets
(transvestite)**
Alcazar Cabaret
Pattaya 2 Rd.
Tel: 0 3841 0505.
Tiffany's
Pattaya Sports Bazaar
Bldg, Pattaya 2 Rd.
Tel: 0 3842 1700.

Discos
Captain's Club
Dusit Resort, North
Pattaya Rd.
Tel: 0 3842 9901.
**Marine Bar and
Discotheque**
South Pattaya Rd.
Pattaya Palladeum
Pattaya 2 Rd, (Soi 1).

PHUKET
Bars and pubs
Boathouse Inn
Exclusive. Fine setting.
Kata Beach.
Tel: 0 7633 0015.
Green Man English Pub
Patak Rd, Chalong.
Tel: 0 7628 0757.

Mambo Beach Club
Thaweewong Rd,
Patong.
Tel: 0 7629 2883.
**No Idea Cocktail
Lounge**
89/49 Soi Post Office,
Patong Beach.

Discos
Banana Disco
Patong Beach Hotel,
Thawiwong Rd.
Tel: 0 7634 0301.
Safari Pub and Disco
Patong Beach.
Tel: 0 7634 1310.
Shark Disco
Rat-U-Thit Rd.
Tel: 0 7634 0525.

Facing page and above: dancers performing at a winter fair in Lamphun

the fingers (there are some 200 different movements) takes years to perfect. Hardly surprising, then, that most dancers begin training at the age of six and do not go on stage until they are 15.

Ancient art forms

The dance that most visitors are likely to come across is the masked *khon* dance, where the actors wear glittering costumes covered with gold braid and jewels, as well as magnificent papier mâché masks.

Around the country, there are other dances too. In the south, especially, the Manohra dance, which traditionally tells the tale of a half-bird, half-woman, is popular. There is even a derivative known as the 'Flowerpot Dance', introduced during the reign of King Rama I and modified into the 'Lantern Dance' by one of his regal successors.

Story lines

Classical dances almost inevitably come from the famous legend known as the *Ramakien*, which is the Thai name for the great Hindu *Ramayana* epic. The legend tells of young Prince Rama who is banished from the kingdom of Ayodhya but, after numerous adventures and the intervention of the monkey king Hanuman, returns triumphantly to his court where, as in all fairy tales, he lives happily ever after.

You will not get much information from the dancers, though. Characters do not speak, and only rarely does the scenery change. Even identifying them depends on recognising the colours of the costumes they wear. There is normally, however, a narrator or chorus

Thai *likay* performances are very popular

Thai drama and dancing

Thai classical dancing is a beautiful and exotic spectacle that no visitor should miss. In the old days, a full performance could take up to a week and include as many as 300 characters, made up of gods, demons, giants, monkeys and angels. These days, it is generally shortened to a couple of hours, highlighting just a few episodes. This is still enough to give an idea both of the rich variety and skill involved.

Indeed, so complex and demanding are the roles that even the simple use of

that sings along, providing an outline of the plot, and accompanied by a *piphat* (gong and xylophone) orchestra. The music is specifically geared towards the action, with some 200 different tunes each denoting a different mood; one for anger, another for love, a third for betrayal.

Sometimes, even that can be hard to absorb. But, as an acquired taste, Thai dancing is said to be like caviar. Once you have got a taste for it, you will not want anything else.

Likay

Any account of classical dance would be incomplete without a mention of *likay*, the indomitable pantomime that sprang up during the reign of King Chulalongkorn.

Whereas classical dance was originally aimed at the aristocracy, *likay* is acted out for the local people. You may see it at a street fair or even at a funeral. Especially popular in rural areas, it tends to be brassy and crude, bawdy and suggestive, but wherever it goes, it continues to captivate the hearts of the people.

Performance venues in Bangkok
Baan Thai Restaurant *7 Sukhumvit Soi 32. Tel: 0 2258 5403.*
Maneeya's Lotus Room *Phloen Chit Rd. Tel: 0 2252 6312.*
National Theatre *Na Phra That Rd. Tel: 0 2224 1342.*
Ruen Thep Restaurant *Silom Village Trade Centre, Silom Rd. Tel: 0 2233 9447.*
Sala Rim Naam *Oriental Hotel, Charoen Nakom Rd. Tel: 0 2437 9417.*
Thailand Cultural Centre *Ratchadaphisek Rd, Huai Khwang. Tel: 0 2247 0028.*

Candles play a dominant part in many forms of Thai dance and drama

Children

Bringing children to Thailand may seem like hard work, but there are plenty of compensations, such as friendly childminders, excellent hotels and good medical services. There are also plenty of sights to see, both in Bangkok and around the country, that will appeal to children and to their parents. Be sure that your children have the necessary injections, provide them with hats and sunglasses, and keep them out of the sun. Apart from these precautions, there is no reason why a visit to Thailand should not be, for them, the holiday of a lifetime.

TEN MAIN ATTRACTIONS FOR CHILDREN

1 Boat trip on Bangkok's Chao Phraya River (*see pp56–7*).
2 Bangkok's Snake Farm (*see pp42–3*).
3 Crocodile Farm at Samut Prakan (*see p60*).
4 Elephant Farm at Mae Taeng (*see p83*).
5 Floating market at Damnoen Saduak (*see p61*).
6 Hill-tribe village at Ban Doi Pui (*see p80*).
7 National Park at Khao Yai (*see p63*).
8 Seaside at Phuket (*see p116*).
9 Tham Pla (Fish Cave) at Mae Hong Son (*see p91*).
10 Umbrella factories on San Kamphaeng Rd, Chiang Mai (*see p72*).

BANGKOK AND SURROUNDINGS

Ancient City: Scaled-down models of temples and monuments found all over the country (*see p60*).
Dream World: 28-hectare entertainment centre. *Rangsit Nakhonyok Rd. Tel: 0 2533 1152. Admission charge.*
Dusit Zoo: More than 500 animals including snakes and elephants (*see p32*).
Kite-flying: During spring weekends at Sanam Luang (*see p160*).
Lumphini Park: Pedal boats, walks and ice creams in the centre of town (*see p39*).
Planetarium: *928 Sukhumvit Rd. Tel: 0 2392 1773. Open: Tue–Sun 8.30am–4pm. Admission charge.*

The Rose Garden: Lush resort to the west of Bangkok with daily shows, tribal dances and beautiful gardens (*see p69*).

CHIANG MAI AND THE NORTH

Chiang Mai Zoo: Largest Zoo in Thailand (*see p71*).
Doi Suthep Temple: Up in the hills with excellent views of Chiang Mai (*see p80*).
Mae Sa Valley: Orchid, snake and elephant farms, and waterfalls within easy distance of town (*see p82*).

PATTAYA AND THE GULF

Elephant Village: Elephant shows and rides (*see p106*).
Khao Khieo Open Zoo: 40 hectares of forest, aviary, waterfalls and wildlife (*see p107*).

Ko Lan Island: Picturesque island with beaches and restaurants reached by boat (*see p106*).

Nong Nooch Village: 220 hectares of exotic gardens; daily cultural shows with Thai dancing (*see p107*).

Ocean World: Water slides, bumper cars, amusement park (*see p108*).

Pattaya Park: Big swimming pool, waterchutes and whirlpool within easy reach of Pattaya (*see p107*).

PHUKET AND THE SOUTH

Aquarium: Over 100 species of fish on display, together with various crustaceans and other marine life (*see p113*).

Beaches: Kata and Karon beaches on Phuket (*see p116*). Chaweng beach on Ko Samui (*see p126*).

James Bond Island: Weird limestone formations and spangled islands at Phang Nga, off Phuket (*see p118*).

Nakha Noi Pearl Farm: Home of the largest grown cultured pearl in the world (*see p118*).

Mai Khao Beach: This is where the sea turtles come ashore from November to February each year, to lay their eggs (*see p117*).

Native children even ride water buffalo, but it's not recommended for the amateur

Sport and leisure

Given the heat, the rain and the humidity, you might think that sport and Thailand were incompatible. In fact, neither the elements nor Bangkok's traffic and pollution have dinted local appetites for outdoor and indoor exertion.

Golf, tennis, and sailing are now so well established that new clubs are even taking precedence over traditional sports, while even in the heat of a Bangkok evening, crowds can be seen running around the parks, rolling tyres, and practising *tae kwon do* (martial arts).

A fitness centre in a Bangkok hotel

Fitness centres

Fitness centres, weight rooms and saunas are found in most big hotels. Bangkok, especially, offers plenty of choice. The **Dusit Thani Hotel** (*Rama IV Rd, tel: 0 2236 0450*), the **Menam Riverside Hotel** (*Charoen Krung Rd, tel: 0 2688 1000*) and the **Landmark Hotel** (*Sukhumvit Rd, tel: 0 2254 0404*) all have facilities open to non-hotel guests. The **Oriental Hotel** (*tel: 0 2659 9000*), **Shangri-La Hotel** (*tel: 0 2236 7777*) and the **Siam Inter-Continental Hotel** (*tel: 0 2253 0355*) have gyms reserved for hotel guests only.

Outside Bangkok, a number of resorts and hotels also have facilities, especially in Phuket and Pattaya. Enquire at offices of the Tourist Authority of Thailand (TAT) for details.

Golf

One of the great newly discovered paradises for golfers, Thailand's greens are now attracting the sort of attention that only a few years ago was reserved for its beaches. Its secret? Good weather, challenging courses, cheap caddies, low fees and easy access.

In all, the country has more than 50 courses. Generally, these will rent out golf clubs and balls, although you should always check before you leave home.

Local courses within reach of Bangkok are the **Navatanee** (*tel: 0 2376 1034*), **Krungthep Kritha** (*tel: 0 2379 3716*), the **Rose Garden** (*tel: 0 3432 2769*) and **Unico** (*tel: 0 2377 9038*). Outside Bangkok some of the best golf courses are the **Royal Hua Hin Golf Course** at Hua Hin (*tel: 0 3251 2475*), the **Lanna Golf Club** in Chiang Mai (*tel: 0 5322 1911*), and the **Phuket Golf and Country Club** at Phuket (*tel: 0 7632 1039*).

Weekday rates range from 650 baht to 2,500 baht for a round of 18 holes, although costs are higher at weekends. Caddies generally cost in the region of 300 baht. Most clubs have restaurants, bars and often accommodation. Always book in advance, especially at weekends when clubs are most popular.

Horse racing and riding

Unexpected it may be, but Bangkok has two full-sized racecourses. This may have more to do with the Thai propensity for betting than with their love of horses, but it is enough to make horse racing especially popular. Races take place at the **Royal Turf Club** (*183 Phitsanulok Rd, tel: 0 2280 0020*), and at the **Royal Bangkok Sports Club** (*tel: 0 2251 0181*) on alternate Sundays. Both clubs have membership enclosures. Outside, there are also public stands where the gambling can be seen.

For those wanting to ride, the centres outside Bangkok are: **Phuket Riding Club** (*Chalong, tel: 0 7628 8213*), and **Pattaya's Reo Ranch** which offers 6km (4 miles) of trail-rides on thoroughbreds imported from Australia.

Swimming and tennis

All the big hotels have swimming pools and even the medium-sized hotels have small pools. Outside that, there are few public baths save for Bangkok's **YMCA** (*27 Sathorn Tai Road, tel: 0 2677 6240; open: daily 7am–7pm*).

For tennis courts try Bangkok's **Ambassador Hotel**, the **Shangri-La Hotel**, and the **Imperial Queens Park Hotel**, as well as the **Central Tennis Courts** (*13/1 Soi Attakarnprasit, Sathorn Tai Rd, tel: 0 2286 7202*), and **Soi Klang Racquet Club** (*8 Soi 49, Sukhumvit*).

The country has some spectacular golf courses

TRADITIONAL THAI SPORTS

From Thai-style boxing to fighting fish and kite-flying, the Thais appear to have an unquenchable relish for unusual athletic and spectator sports. The origin of some of these sports can be traced back centuries, and they remain a strong form of local entertainment, and are a major source of betting.

Fighting fish

This is not really a sport, nor is it even legal, but fighting fish (the species *Bettas spendens*) continue to provide one of the most popular and unusual activities in the country. The game begins when two males are put together in a tank or basin after bets have been taken.

The fight can last for seconds or for hours and only comes to an end when one of the fish dies or flees to a corner. Although officially banned in Thailand, fights can be widely seen. Elsewhere, cricket fights, bullfights, and cockfights attract an equal outpouring of bets.

Kite-flying

When the skies are clear and the wind is up, the popular kite-flying season gets underway.

Most fliers participate in a competition, the aim of which is to try and snare the line of an opponent's kite with their own, and then pull the enemy kite across a capture line marked on the ground.

At weekends, especially between February and April, Sanam Luang, opposite Bangkok's Grand Palace, is a solid mass of colours as kites of all shapes and sizes bob around the sky. Occasionally, Thailand even holds international competitions to find the world's best kite-flier.

Longboat racing

Longboat racing, one of the country's oldest sports, dates back to the Ayutthaya period (14th to 18th century) and can still be seen, if you are lucky, on a few rare occasions.

Races are held under Bangkok's Rama IX Bridge on the Chao Phraya River, normally in the month of September. In the provinces, the towns of Nan, Nakhon Phanom and Pichit also hold their own races, scheduled between the months of September and November.

TRADITIONAL MASSAGE

Tense? Exhausted? A traditional massage could be just the thing. Thai massage traces its roots back hundreds of years, owing its existence to the great Indian civilisation. It involves applying pressure to certain points within the body.

To experience it as it should be, visit **Wat Pho** (*see p49*), the home of traditional massage. Other places in Bangkok include the **Marble House** (*37/18 Soi Surawong Plaza, tel: 0 2235 2148*), and **Buathip Thai Massage** (*4/13 Sukhumvit Soi 5 opposite the Landmark Hotel, tel: 0 2255 1045*).

Outside these veritable establishments, massage tends to be less traditional and more costly.

Muay Thai

This is the most popular spectator sport in Thailand, and the biggest crowd-puller in the capital. *Muay Thai,* or Thai-style boxing, has not become a big hit without good reason.

Like normal boxing, it involves two opponents wearing gloves, but, unlike normal boxing, competitors can use their feet, fists, knees and elbows to batter each other into submission. Bouts consist of five three-minute rounds accompanied by traditional Thai music and frantic betting, especially among the third-class ticket holders. Such is the demand that there are normally at least 10 bouts in any night's programme.

Thai boxing is held in Bangkok at the **Ratchadamnoen Stadium** (*Ratchadamnoen Nok Ave, tel: 0 2281 4205*) on Mondays, Wednesdays, Thursdays, and Sundays, or at the **Lumphini Boxing Stadium** (*Rama IV Rd near park, tel: 0 2251 4303*). Prices range from 150 baht for third-class seats to over 1,000 baht for a top ringside seat. Seats are generally available on the night and do not require booking, but those interested should get there early.

Takraw

This popular sport is also played in Myanmar and Malaysia. Requiring great skill, it uses a small, hollow rattan ball. Players must neither touch the ball with their hands, nor allow it to touch the ground. Elbows, shoulders and the back of the head can be used. The more complicated the feat, the better the score. Played by six to seven men, a version known as hoop *takraw* is the most popular. During a 30-minute game, each man cooperates with another in order to earn a high score. Played without nets, the ball passes from player to player, and each scores according to his dexterity. Net *takraw* matches can be seen at the National Stadium in Bangkok. In the country you will see people playing it in the evenings.

Kite-flying is a pastime enjoyed by young and old

WATERSPORTS

Once sand and blue seas were enough to attract visitors to Thailand. Now it is the things that go with them: the parasailing and game-fishing, the sailing and waterskiing. These are aimed at visitors of all skill levels, and in all price ranges, and can be arranged either by your hotel or on the beach itself.

Main centres are Phuket, Pattaya and Ko Samui. Krabi and Ko Phi Phi are beginning to offer more extensive facilities. Wherever you are, and whatever people tell you to the contrary, always check on safety standards, and always ask for official certification. It may not be much, but it could just save your skin.

All sports, including paragliding, are popular in the jet-set resorts of Pattaya and Phuket

Deep-sea fishing

Increasingly popular, deep-sea fishing is now available in many forms to suit the amateur or the specialist. The best centres are Phuket and Jomtien, where catches range from blue marlin to barracuda. When you have hooked your fish, you can take it to a nearby restaurant, where they will turn it into some local delicacy. Phuket is coming up with more companies offering overnight expeditions.

Paragliding

Paragliding, the sport of jumping into the air behind a speedboat, suspended from a kite, may not be everyone's idea of fun, but it is the latest hit sport to come Thailand's way. Almost all the big island resorts now offer facilities; indeed, in Pattaya and on Phuket's Patong Beach, paragliding is so popular that people just wanting to sunbathe or paddle hardly get a look in. Official instructors will show you the ropes. Be warned, however, that there have been accidents. Check out the situation before you get up there.

Sailing

From 30-m (98-ft) sailing cruisers and catamarans to small hobbies and dinghies, Thailand has just about every form of motorised, sail-based and oar-propelled water transport.

The big centres are Phuket and Pattaya. Make sure that you book in advance, especially during the high season. The following organise trips:

East West Siam
70/176 Paradise Complex, Rat-U-Thit Road, Patong Beach. Tel: 0 7634 0912; www.ewsiam.com

Yachtpro International
57/5 Moo 2 Mai Khao. Tel: 0 7634 8117; www.sailing-thailand.com

Scuba-diving

Visitors who come to Thailand specifically to dive may still be in the minority, but they represent a growing number. The chief destinations are Phuket, Pattaya and Krabi, although the lesser known Similan and Surin Islands also offer colourful coral reefs and underwater marine life. Good, sheltered water is generally found around the islands at any time of year (although during the monsoon the water becomes cloudy), and boats are readily available to take you out there. For those with no previous experience, scuba-diving courses are offered at Phuket and Pattaya; as well as catering for beginners, there are also courses for advanced divers. Alternatively, equipment can be hired at numerous shops along the beach. For those with lesser ambitions, snorkels and face masks are also widely available. The best months for diving near Phuket are November to April.

From June to November during the southwest monsoon, the area can be tricky and visibility poor.

The following firms hire out equipment and offer diving instruction:

Andaman Divers
Patong Beach, Phuket. Tel: 0 7634 1126; www.andamandivers.com

Samui International Diving School
Ko Samui. Tel: 0 7742 2386; www.planet-scuba.net

Sea Bees Diving
Chalong Bay, Phuket. Tel: 0 7638 1765; www.sea-bees.com

Windsurfing

Windsurfers who come to Thailand will not find the surf of Kuta Beach, nor the boards of Hawaii, but windsurfing is on the increase, and popular spots are to be found in Jomtien, Phuket and Ko Samui. Windsurfing boards can be rented on a daily basis. Enquire at any of the beaches for details.

The clear turquoise waters off Phuket are perfect for scuba-diving

Food and drink

To the great culinary nations of the world there has been added a new and rising star. Thailand is no longer just a third-world market stall, but an exciting experience for connoisseurs, with new Thai restaurants springing up in large numbers around the world, as well as recipe books and cooking courses taking up its cause. Thai food encapsulates an enormous variety of tastes and spices ranging from the glutinous rice of the northeast, to the pungent curries of the south. It brings together some of the finest cooking traditions from all over Asia. Above all, it is a celebration by people who love their food, and who count eating as one of the great pleasures in life.

A tempting display of Thai cuisine

A touch of spice

Thai food can be spicy or mild, but it is never purely and simply hot. Numerous spices are used to enhance the flavour and to improve the taste, but never to conceal it.

The blend of ingredients partly reflects the historical mix of the people themselves. Thai food is a combination of various cuisines, including Indian, Malay, Chinese and Indonesian.

The most important spice for any dish is chilli. *Phrik leuang* is the hottest chilli, despite its lovely yellow-orange colour. *Phrik khi nu* is not so potent, while *phrik yuak* and *phrik chi fa* are relatively mild.

But there is far more to Thai cooking than chillies. Coriander is sprinkled on meats, along with garlic and pepper, to enhance the taste. Ginger and tamarind add further flavour, along with mint, basil, cardamom and galanga. Lemon-grass, a spice used extensively in soups and salads, adds a certain piquancy, while many dishes use coconut milk and pineapple, adding a mellowness, cooling the palate, and complementing the other spices.

Playing the gourmet

About the only requirement demanded by Thai food is that you should enjoy it. Beyond that, eat it how you want, when you want, and with what you want. There is no need for knives, nor even for bowls, and if you swallow a chilli, don't worry about convention – just dive for the rice bowl or a glass of water.

Thais do, however, follow a few guidelines. They almost always order a selection of dishes and share them. As an accompaniment they will almost always have rice. In principle, they will choose a balanced range of dishes – fish, meat, curry and vegetables.

Finally, you will find that locals generally wash down a good Thai meal with either *mekong* (rice-based) whisky or beer, but rarely wine. Vintage wine is considered extravagant and ill-suited to the flavours of Thai food. Generally, a bottle would also cost more than the whole meal.

A typical menu

A typical menu will usually include a *tom yam* (hot) soup, a spicy salad (*yam*), a curry (*gaeng*) and a fried fish (*pla tod*). For variety there may be a chicken in pandanus leaves (*gai haw bai toey*), as well as a coconut-based broth (*tom ka gai*), and some fried vegetables (*phak phat ruam mit*).

For those who like food unflavoured by chillies, ask for *mai phet* (not hot). Order a sweet-and-sour fish (*pla priew wan*) or roast duck (*phet tod*), some noodles (*mi krop*), or a plate of fried rice with chicken (*khao phat kai*). For dessert, the Thais favour dishes that foreigners often find excessively sweet. They are called *khanom*, and may vary from riceflour and coconut milk to sticky rice and custard. If you do not have a sweet tooth it is safer to ask for *ponlamai* (fresh fruits), and eat bananas, pineapples or the exotic mangosteen.

Other cuisines

Excellent Thai food there may be in abundance, but that does not stop those with a taste for other foods from enjoying excellent Chinese, Vietnamese and European-style cuisine.

These restaurants are now found throughout Bangkok, as well as in Chiang Mai, Phuket, Pattaya and Ko Samui.

A Thai meal is usually well balanced and beautifully presented

The local touch

A sense of adventure and an expectation of the unusual are two qualities that any potential diner should have. For Thais enjoy several dishes which as yet go unappreciated by the Western palate. Snake's blood is one of the most consummate delicacies. The blood of cobras, kraits and vipers, served up by mobile snake shops at Lumphini Park, is not only delicious, but is said to be the secret of eternal life and vitality.

Field rats and fried grasshoppers also provide wholesome snacks, while water buffalo is eaten almost everywhere, even in many restaurants around Bangkok.

Finally, there is another delicacy that you should not turn your nose up at – waterbeetles (*mengda*), are especially prized. Eaten raw (only the female), three can cost as much as 20 baht – but such is their quality, they are considered a snack in themselves.

Going regional

Wherever you go in Thailand you are likely to get curry, *tom yam* soup, or the omnipresent *khao phat kai* (fried rice), though the regional specialities of some areas are particularly well known.

Anyone visiting the northeast has to try *larb*, a dish made from water buffalo, pork or beef, fried with garlic, chillies and shallots, and served with cabbage and mint, or with *khao niao*, a form of glutinous rice. Also not to be missed is *somtam*, made from shredded green papaya, dried shrimps, lemon juice, garlic and chilli – the perfect antidote to any cold.

In the deep south, food tends to be hotter, with such ferociously piquant dishes as *kaeng leuang* (yellow curry) and *kaeng tai pla* (fish kidney curry). If you do not like hot foods it is safer to opt for fresh prawns, seafood cooked in coconut milk, or Phuket lobster.

Khantoke dinners

Visitors to Chiang Mai may well find themselves confronted, at some stage, with the dinner known as *khantoke*. This is a traditional banquet comprising several dishes, including a thick pork curry spiced with garlic and ginger, minced pork

LIQUID REFRESHMENTS

Almost all drinks that are available in the West can be found in Thailand.

Water is bought in bottles, although restaurants and cafés will almost always boil their own.

There is a variety of local beers, including Kloster and Singha, which are quite palatable.

Wine is available in the more up-market restaurants but at quite high prices.

The most popular drink in the land is *mekong*, a rice-based whisky, which is definitely not for the faint-hearted.

cooked with tomatoes and chillies, fried pork skin, chicken and vegetable curry, and minced meat mixed with chillies. It is delicious.

Street stalls

An indefinable urge to binge, combined with apprehension, is the usual reaction to a wagon loaded with succulent grilled kebabs.

But it is here that you will find some of the best regional and local food; luscious pieces of chicken, or steaming bowls of noodles, piping-hot soups with fish, or tangy sausages flavoured with herbs and pork and stuffed with rice.

Do not ignore them. Although you should go easy on the stomach, especially in the first few days of your visit, be aware that these are some of the best, cheapest and most delicious foods that Thailand has on offer.

Fruits

Whatever time of the year you are in Thailand, you will come across some of the most sumptuous and exotic fruits in the world. The most prized is the durian, a fruit that resembles a green hedgehog, and smells like a rubbish tip but tastes great.

Then there are pineapples and coconuts, papayas and mangoes, along with the sweet, translucent flesh of rambutans, and small, sweet custard apples. Finally, there are grapes, strawberries, apples, more than ten kinds of banana, and even a type of tangerine known as *som* which is widely grown.

Ducks are a popular delicacy

Where to eat

Eating in Thailand is usually very cheap. A good Thai meal will generally cost less than 350 baht a head (excluding alcohol). Only if you eat in European restaurants in the big hotels will the cost be much higher.

In the restaurant listings below, the following symbols have been used to indicate the average cost per person, not including alcohol:

★   100–300 baht
★★   300–500 baht
★★★   500–900 baht

Service is generally charged at the rate of 10 per cent in the bigger restaurants. Elsewhere it is generally sufficient to leave 30 baht on the table.

BANGKOK
Thai food
Baan Khanitha ★★★
A classic Thai restaurant set in a beautiful old house.
36/1 Sukhumvit Soi 23.
Tel: 0 2258 4181.
Bussaracum ★★★
One of Bangkok's best-known classical Thai restaurants.
139 Sethiwan Tower, Pan Rd. Tel: 0 2266 6312.

Sala Rim Nam ★★★
Exclusive dining by the river with classical dancing.
Oriental Hotel, Charoen Krung Rd.
Tel: 0 2659 9000;
www.mandarin oriental.com
Silom Village (Ruen Thep) ★★
Good food and *gamelan* (gong) music within easy reach of shops.
286 Silom Rd.
Tel: 0 2234 4448.
Thanying ★★
Good Thai cuisine in beautifully decorated house.
10 Pramuan Rd, Silom.
Tel: 0 2236 4361.
Whole Earth Restaurant ★
Vegetarian and Thai food to the sound of classical guitar.
93/3 Soi Langsuan, Phloen Chit Rd.
Tel: 0 2252 5574.

International food
Le Banyan ★★★
Classic French restaurant.
59 Sukhumvit Soi 8.
Tel: 0 2253 5556.
El Gordo's ★★
Best Mexican restaurant in town.
130/8 Soi 8 Silom Rd.
Tel: 0 2234 5470.

Haus Munchen ★★
German specialities.
4 Sukhumvit 15.
Tel: 0 2252 5776.
La Normandie ★★★
Most expensive and exclusive French food in town.
Oriental Hotel, Charoen Krung Rd.
Tel: 0 2659 9000;
www.mandarin oriental.com
L'Opera ★★★
Top Italian specialities.
53 Sukhumvit Soi 39.
Tel: 0 2258 5606.

Floating restaurants
Pearl of Siam ★★★
Nightly candle-lit dinner cruises.
Operated by Shangri-La Hotel. Tel: 0 2255 9200.
Tahsaneeya Nava (Loy Nava) ★★
One of the oldest and most elegant riverside restaurants.
Tel: 0 2437 4932.

CHIANG MAI
Thai food
Baan Suan Restaurant ★★
Delicious food, delightful grounds.
51/3 San Kamphaeng Rd.
Tel: 0 5326 2568.
Riverside Bar and Restaurant ★★
Thai and European food, live bands.

9/11 Charoen Rat Rd.
Tel: 0 5324 3239.
Whole Earth
Restaurant ★★
Vegetarian and northern
food in teak-wood
house.
88 Sridonchai Rd.
Tel: 0 5328 2463.

Khantoke dinners
Banquets in the
northern style
(*see pp166–7*).
Baan Suan Restaurant ★
Chiang Inn Plaza,
100/1 Chang Khlan Rd.
Tel: 0 5328 3094.
Diamond Hotel ★★★
33/10 Charoen
Prathet Rd.
Tel: 0 5327 2080.
Old Chiang Mai
Cultural Centre ★★★
185/3 Wua Lai Rd.
Tel: 0 5320 2993.

International food
Le Coq d'Or ★★★
Best French cuisine.
11 Soi 2 Koh Klang Rd.
Tel: 0 5328 2024.
German Hofbrauhaus
Y Casa Antonio ★★
German food.
115/1-2 Loi Kroh Rd.
Tel: 0 5382 1273.
Heuan Phen ★
Northern Thai food.
112 Ratchamankha Rd.
Tel: 0 5327 7103.

PATTAYA
Thai food
PIC Kitchen ★★
Tropical gardens.
Excellent food.
Soi 5, Beach Rd, North
Pattaya.
Tel: 0 3842 8387;
www.pic-kitchen.com
Ruen Thai ★★
Traditional restaurant
with classical dancing.
485/3 Pattaya 2 Rd.
Tel: 0 3842 5911.

International food
El Toro Steakhouse ★★
A good selection of steaks
and hors d'oeuvres is
served here.
214/31–32, Pattaya 2 Rd.
Tel: 0 3842 6238.
La Gritta ★★★
Authentic Italian
food accompanied by
pianist.
North Beach Rd.
Tel: 0 3842 8161;
www.amari.com
Lobster Pot BT★
Seafood served from old
fishermen's wharf.
228 Beach Rd,
opposite Soi 14.
Tel: 0 3842 6083.
Noble House
Restaurant ★★
A varied selection of
European, Thai and
Chinese dishes.
310 Beach Rd South,
Tel: 0 3842 3630.

PHUKET
Thai food
Baan Rim Pa ★★★
Traditional teak-wood
house with top gourmet
cooking.
100/7 Kalim Beach Rd,
Patong Beach.
Tel: 0 7634 0789;
www.baanrimpa.com
Old Siam ★★★
Great Thai food and
wonderful views.
Karon Beach.
Tel: 0 7639 6090.
Prantalay ★★
One of Phuket's best fish
restaurants, with first-
class views.
Soi Palai, Chalong Bay.
Tel: 0 7638 3243.

International food
Le Jardin ★★
Good French food in
the heart of the night
scene.
Soi Bangla,
Patong Beach.
Tel: 0 7629 2331.
Karon Cafe ★★
Great choice of
international cuisine.
Karon Circle.
Tel: 0 7639 6217;
www.karoncafe.com
Molly Malones Irish
Pub ★★
Good value for money.
68 Thaweewong Rd,
Patong.
Tel: 0 7629 2771.

Hotels and accommodation

Thailand is justifiably ranked as having some of the finest hotels in the world. Names like the Oriental, the Peninsula and the Shangri-La now pop up regularly among the top international reviews, and are just as pricey as elsewhere. But the characteristic *namchai* (hospitality) does not necessarily stop in the top slot. Numerous smaller and cheaper establishments offer the sort of service that, in the West, would cost an arm and a leg – and even the backpacker is not forgotten.

Keep mobility in mind when choosing a hotel

Most visitors book accommodation prior to departure, but before signing on the dotted line, find out exactly what you are in for. Hotels may have swimming pools and restaurants, but if they are a long way from the centre of town you could find your movements considerably restricted, bearing in mind Thai traffic jams. Those who do not book a room prior to arrival can generally find the full range of accommodation on offer (and generally at cheaper rates than back home). At certain times of year, however, a reservation is a definite advantage, if not a must. In Phuket and Ko Samui during Christmas and the New Year, hotels are reserved months in advance.

Dos and don'ts

Room prices in Thailand usually include a 10–15 per cent service charge, local hotel tax, and 7 per cent tax; always enquire before you book.

During the low season (March to September) hotels may offer special rates. Some international travel agencies these days are also able to offer very substantial discounts, either as part of a package tour, or for a short stopover on the way to some other Asian or Antipodean destination.

Bear in mind the following points when selecting your hotel. Stay clear of hotels situated next to a building site or undergoing renovation (workmen are at it 24 hours a day), especially in Bangkok, but these days in Phuket and Pattaya as well. Similarly, avoid hotels located on main roads. Also keep in mind that there are some establishments that double as brothels.

Do not drink tap water. Big hotels provide mineral water in fridges; cheaper hotels, jugs of boiled water. Tip the staff if they provide excellent service or if you are staying in a luxury hotel, but remember that 20–50 baht is fine. Always check that your door or window is secure and, if you are staying in a bungalow, bring a padlock.

Finally, remember that phone calls and hotel meals are expensive. Also put things in perspective: hotels in Bangkok may provide a pleasant interlude, but the real Thailand is generally found outside, in the streets and market stalls, and in the delightful little restaurants.

Off the beaten track

When you are off the main tourist routes, do not expect to find the same sort of accommodation that you would find in the major tourist centres. In small towns, hotels may be located in beautiful old Chinese wooden houses, in simple guesthouses or pretty basic hostels. Sometimes you may have no choice at all and all that's available is a disreputable bar.

Always try to arrive during daylight. The moment you arrive, start looking around. If you are stuck, ask at the police station (*satanee tamruat*) or at the bus station. If you are still stuck, go to the local *wat* (temple) and ask for permission to stay. Be sure to make a donation when you leave.

Remember that the word for hotel is *rong raem,* and for guest house *ge how* (similar to the English words, but Thais find it difficult to pronounce 'st').

In general, you should be able to find some sort of accommodation almost anywhere, though it may not be what you want, and it may not have a private bathroom. But if that bothers you, you should stay in one of the main centres.

New wooden accommodation at Ko Samui

Prices and facilities

What you get for your money is likely to depend as much on when you come, as how you arrange it. During the popular tourist months, from November through to February, room rates are generally around 30+ per cent higher, although it is always worth checking out several agents and hotels.

Four- and five-star accommodation

Top-quality hotels in Thailand offer all the amenities that you would find anywhere in the world. Fine restaurants, discotheques, cocktail lounges and other entertainment facilities are generally provided, along with business facilities, fax services and IDD telephones. Some hotels provide special secretarial services, and almost all of them have 24-hour room service. The luxury hotel sector is the one that has grown fastest in recent years. In theory, this should mean cheaper rates, but it has yet to be reflected in prices.

The reception at Amity Green Hills, Chiang Mai

Rooms at the Oriental, Bangkok's best-known riverside hotel, range from a normal room to the Royal Suite, and accordingly room rates vary greatly. At the nearby Shangri-La, prices are slightly lower and, as with most hotel room rates in Bangkok, are often quoted in US dollars.

Hotels outside Bangkok tend to be cheaper, with an excellent standard of accommodation in Chiang Mai, Chiang Rai, the Golden Triangle, Mae Hong Son, Phuket, Ko Samui, Hua Hin and Pattaya.

Any luxury hotel should be able to advise you on tours, as well as arranging chauffeurs, transfer to the airport, or any other travel requirement.

Many local hotel chains offer a range of good-value, four-star accommodation to suit both business and leisure travellers. They have hotels in Bangkok, Chiang Mai, beach resorts in Pattaya, Phuket and Samui.

Standard accommodation

General standards of hotels in the middle group are high, prices are relatively cheap, while the food and service are more than adequate – though without the attention to detail that is found in the more upper-crust establishments. Most of the hotels in this range offer facilities such as swimming pools as well as a restaurant, bar, travel desk and room service. Rooms are air-conditioned, and almost all have safes where you can leave your valuables.

Prices in Bangkok vary from 850 baht at the **YMCA** to 8,000 baht plus at up-market hotels. In the provinces, or on

Courtesy and friendliness make Thailand's hospitality industry one of the best in the world

the islands, standard accommodation offers good, clean and (by Western standards) exceptionally cheap rooms. This is especially true of Ko Samui, with good bungalows costing upwards of 1,000 baht. In Phuket, however, they tend to cost considerably more.

Budget accommodation

One thing Thailand does not lack is cheap accommodation. Small rooms in big hotels, grubby rooms in grubby hotels, spartan guest houses, private homes – all these cater to the budget traveller. Budget accommodation in Bangkok begins at Khao San Road, the backpackers' street in downtown Banglampoo, that has become known the world over. A bed in a dormitory can be had for as little as 150 baht, and

single rooms for upwards of 250 baht. Most guest houses have communal bathrooms and small restaurants, although the vast number of such places means that there is generally something available to suit every need.

More up-market versions of Khao San Road are found throughout Bangkok, though at generally higher prices. One of the most popular establishments is the top end Malaysia Hotel, with prices ranging from 500 baht upwards.

In the provinces, prices for a room in a guest house start at around 300 baht, although you may have to pay considerably more in Phuket. Theft from budget accommodation is by no means unknown. Always take precautions, not only against outsiders, but also against your fellow travellers.

Practical guide

Arriving
Entry formalities
Visitors from most countries will need a visa to stay in Thailand for more than 30 days. All passports must be valid for at least six months beyond the date of departure from Thailand.

Visas may also be issued for 30 days (transit visa), for 60 days (tourist visa), and for 90 days (non-immigrant visa). They are obtainable from all Thai embassies and consulates abroad.

Extensions of tourist and non-immigrant visas can be requested at the Immigration Division, Bangkok, or at other immigration centres throughout the country. Travellers staying for less than 30 days without a visa must be in possession of confirmed onward/return air tickets. Anyone overstaying their visa is fined 200 baht per day.

By air
Bangkok's Don Muang International Airport is served by more than 40 airlines with frequent flights to and from Europe, North America and Australia. International flights and charter companies also serve Phuket, Hat Yai, Koh Samui and Chiang Mai.

Standards of efficiency at Don Muang are high, both at the airport (which has a duty-free shop) and at Thai International, the national carrier. Book in advance. Flights over Christmas are booked as much as six months earlier. An airport tax of 500 baht is charged at departure for international flights.

The Thomas Cook Worldwide Network Licensee (see p189) will offer airline ticket re-routing and revalidation to travellers who have purchased their travel tickets from Thomas Cook.

Airport transport
To get from Don Muang International Airport to Bangkok, which is situated some 22km (13^1/$_2$ miles) away (average journey time: 45 minutes), catch one of the airport taxis whose drivers wait in the lobby in the arrivals hall. These registered taxis are the form of transport recommended by the tourist authority. Thai Limousine Service is more expensive. Shuttle and ordinary buses also run to the centre.

Trains leave infrequently to Hualamphong railway station but, if you have luggage, it is hardly worth the trouble. Finally, avoid touts who offer to take you independently to your hotel.

Information about arrivals and departures is available 24 hours a day (tel: 0 2535 1111). Lists of airline telephone numbers can be found in most of the free local handout magazines and in the English-language Yellow Pages phone directory.

By rail
Trains link Singapore and Bangkok, with intermediate stops at Kuala Lumpur and Butterworth in Malaysia, and at the southern Thai towns of Hat Yai and Surat Thani (jump-off point for Ko Samui). Journey times from Singapore to Bangkok are approximately 36 hours; from Butterworth to Bangkok, 20 hours.

Sleepers are available, although you should reserve in advance. At the

Malaysian border all passengers must alight to go through immigration.

All trains depart and arrive at Hualamphong Station on Rama IV Rd (*tel: 0 2223 7010/7020*) where there is also a booking office. Advanced tickets can be purchased at all principal stations or at the Bangkok Advanced Booking Office (*tel: 0 2223 3762*).

Train timetables are published in the bi-monthly *Thomas Cook Overseas Timetable*, available from Thomas Cook in the UK (*tel: 01733 416477*), *www.thomascookpublishing.com*

By road
The main overland entry to Thailand consists of three road crossings on the Thai-Malaysian border in Songkhla, Yala and Narathiwat provinces. VIP and air-conditioned buses leave from Singapore, Kuala Lumpur, Butterworth and many intermediate destinations in Malaysia. A road connection to Laos opened a few years ago via the Friendship Bridge.

By sea
There are no regular boat connections to Thailand. Cargo boats calling at Bangkok's Klong Toey port sometimes have passenger cabins. Luxury cruise ships periodically visit Bangkok, Phuket, Ko Samui and Pattaya.

Camping
Some of the islands, including Ko Samet, and a few national parks now have camping facilities. However, camping is not recommended either by the tourist authorities or by the police.

Children
Children under 10, and less than 1m (3ft) tall, can travel free on trains and buses, but are not guaranteed a seat (that is, they must travel seated on their parents' knees if no seats are available). On internal flights, Thai Airways International offers a 50 per cent discount to children under 12, and a 90 per cent discount for those under 2, although you will be required to bring some form of identification.

As a rule, children are extremely well treated throughout the country. Most big hotels have cots, and baby food and nappies are available. For advice about inoculations and medical care, contact your local doctor well before departure.

Climate
Thailand has two distinct climates: tropical in most parts of the country, and tropical monsoon in the southern region. The so-called hot season lasts from March to May and is the least pleasant time to visit. The rainy season, from June to October, has hot, heavy days

Efficient trains cover vast distances in Thailand; the main station in Bangkok is Hualamphong

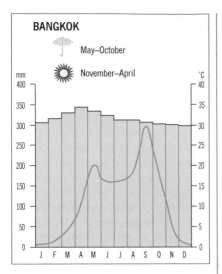

BANGKOK

May–October

November–April

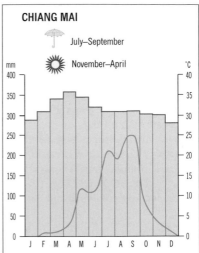

CHIANG MAI

July–September

November–April

Weather Conversion Chart
25.4mm = 1 inch
°F = 1.8 x °C + 32

punctuated by sudden downpours. The cool season, the most popular time to visit, lasts from November to February.

The average temperature in Bangkok is about 27°C (81°F), ranging from 29°C (84°F) in the hottest month of April, to 25°C (77°F) in December. In the north the climate is more temperate, with cool-season temperatures falling to as low as 6°C (48°F).

Clothing

Light, loose cotton clothing is best suited for the climate. Avoid artificial fibres, but bring a sweater if you intend to visit the mountainous areas of the north or northeast during the cool season. Most items of clothing can be purchased easily in Bangkok. See p184 for a conversion table.

Crime

Crime is on the increase in Thailand. Carry only limited amounts of cash on your person, and what you do carry, keep in different pockets. Use a money belt for your passport and credit cards. If you deposit valuables in a hotel safe, get an official receipt in English and an official stamp noting the precise contents. Beware pickpockets and thieves who use razor blades. They are gone before you realise it.

If something is stolen, report the theft immediately to the local police and, if you intend to claim on insurance, get an official document. For Thomas Cook traveller's cheque loss or theft, contact the emergency number (*see p179*).

Finally, never accept gifts of sweets and drinks on trains or buses. There have been numerous cases in which passengers have been drugged and robbed, and the tourist authorities recently issued warnings.

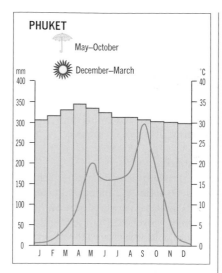

PHUKET

May–October

December–March

Customs regulations

All narcotics (including cannabis, opium, cocaine, morphine and heroin), obscene literature, pictures and articles, and firearms are prohibited. It would be advisable to fully label all tablets and first aid, and to carry proof of purchase with you at all times.

A reasonable amount of clothing for personal use is allowed, along with a litre of spirits and up to 200 cigarettes.

There is no restriction on the import of foreign currency, but amounts over the equivalent of US $10,000 must be declared. Leaving via a neighbouring nation will allow you to take 500,000 baht out of Thailand; otherwise you can only take 50,000 baht out of Thailand.

Buddha images and antiques cannot be taken out of the country without express permission. Some may even need an export licence from the government Fine Arts Department. Shops can arrange this for you.

Driving

Cars and jeeps can be hired by anyone aged over 21 (age limits vary) who possesses a valid driving licence. Those without a driving knowledge of Asia would be unwise to do so. Vehicles drive on the left (generally), but the size of the vehicle is the final arbiter. Trucks often take up the entire road and it is up to you to get out of the way. The speed limit is 50kph in towns, 80kph on highways, and 90kph on expressways, although few people take much notice. Finally, never drive at night.

Petrol and oil are readily available and at prices about 40 per cent of those in Europe.

Renting a car

Most rental firms also operate rescue services. Road signs are generally to the international standard, although directions in the remote provinces may be written exclusively in Thai script.

A sign prohibiting topless bathing

Make sure you have insurance, as many of the smaller hire companies do not include it (*see* Insurance, *pp179–80*). You may also be required to pay a deposit equal to the estimated cost of the rental. Avis and Budget both rent cars and jeeps, and will also be able to arrange chauffeur-driven vehicles.

Avis
(*www.avisthailand.com*)
Bangkok Bangkok International Airport (*tel: 0 2535 4031*); **Chiang Mai** Chiang Mai Airport (*tel: 0 5320 1798*); **Ko Samui** Imperial Samui Hotel (*tel: 0 7742 5031*); **Phuket** opposite Phuket Airport (*tel: 0 7635 1244*).

Budget
(*www.budget.co.th*)
Bangkok Central (*tel: 0 2203 0250*); **Upcountry** Hua Hin, Pattaya, Phuket, Chiang Mai, Udon Thani (*tel: check with Bangkok Central*).

Drugs

Thailand is one of the world's major transit centres for opium and heroin brought in from the Golden Triangle. Never accept a package from any

Two-seater motorbikes are available for hire

stranger, whoever they may claim to be, and never consider smuggling drugs into or out of the country. Just before and after going through customs control, check rucksacks and bags, and let officials see you doing it! Possession or consumption is an extremely serious offence, punishable by life imprisonment or by the death sentence.

Electricity

The standard electric current is 220 volts, 50 cycles AC, although different kinds of sockets are used around the country. Most hotels have a point for shavers, and some have 110-volt sockets. It is best, however, to bring along your own adaptor.

Embassies and consulates

The following is a short list of embassies and consulates in Bangkok. For a full list, see the *Yellow Pages* telephone directory.

Australia
37 Sathorn Tai Rd. Tel: 0 2287 2680.
Canada
15/F, Abdulrahim Place, Rama IV. Tel: 0 2636 0540.
New Zealand
87 Wireless (Witthayu) Rd. Tel: 0 2254 2530.
Republic of Ireland
48/20, 12th Floor, Tisco Tower, North Sathorn Rd. Tel: 0 2638 0303.
UK
1031 Wireless (Witthayu) Rd. Tel: 0 2253 0191.
United States
120–122 Wireless (Witthayu) Rd. Tel: 0 2205 4000.

Emergency telephone numbers
Ambulance: *tel: 0 2255 1133.*
Fire: *tel: 199.*
Highway Police: *tel: 1193 in emergencies,* or *0 2246 0186.*
Police Emergencies: *tel: 191.*
Tourist Police: *tel: 1699 in emergencies.*
Tourist Assistance Centre: *tel: 1155.*

Thomas Cook traveller's cheque loss or theft: UK *tel: 001 44 1733 318950* (reverse charges), or Melbourne, Australia *tel: 001 61 3696 2952* (reverse charges).

MasterCard card loss or theft: *tel: 001 800 11887 0663* (toll free).

Emergency local assistance can also be obtained from Thomas Cook Traveller's Cheques representative office: *8th floor, Bank of Asia Building, 191 South Sathorn Road, Yannawa, Bangkok,* and from Turismo Thai *(see p189).*

Etiquette
Women should never touch a monk. Criticism of the monarchy is not acceptable. Don't go nude bathing, and always wear reasonable clothes when visiting a temple. Photography is prohibited at Don Muang International Airport and at any military installation.

Health
No inoculations or vaccinations are required unless you are coming from or passing through contaminated areas. Yellow fever vaccinations may be required if arriving from an endemic country. However, most doctors advise a boost of typhoid/cholera, malaria tablets, and an optional hepatitis injection. Ask your doctor for advice.

You should also carry a first-aid pack including needles, plasters and iodine.

Never drink tap water (bottled and boiled water is widely available); beware heat exposure (wear a hat); and, most of all, take precautions against venereal and other infectious diseases. Remember that Thailand has a very high number of HIV-positive cases.

All the main hospitals treat urgent medical problems 24 hours a day, although you are expected to pay for treatment on the spot. Provincial towns also usually have reasonably equipped hospitals, though elsewhere facilities are rudimentary.

The following hospitals in Bangkok have emergency departments:
Bangkok Adventist Hospital (24-hour) *430 Phitsanulok Rd. Tel: 0 2281 1422 or 0 2282 1100.*
Bangkok General Hospital *2 Soi Soonwichai, 7 New Phetcha Buri Rd. Tel: 0 2318 0066.*
Police Central *492/1 Ratchadamri Rd, Pathumwan. Tel: 0 2252 8111–25.*
St Louis Hospital *215 South Sathorn Tai Rd. Tel: 0 2675 9300.*
Bangkok also has extremely proficient dentists at low prices.

Hitch-hiking
Hitch-hiking is possible in many of the rural areas but is considered unsafe. Women should never attempt to hitch a lift alone.

Insurance
Insurance is strongly recommended, and should cover you for lost or stolen cash

and credit cards, and guarantee a return ticket in case of emergency. Make sure that you get special cover if items such as cameras exceed the individual limit. Report lost or stolen items to the local police for an officially stamped statement. Without it, insurance firms can refuse to pay claims money.

If you hire a car, collision insurance (collision damage waiver or CDW) is normally offered by the hirer, and is usually compulsory. Check with your own motor insurers if your normal policy covers you. If not, CDW is payable locally, and may be as much as 50 per cent of the hiring fee. Neither CDW nor your personal travel insurance will protect you for liability arising out of an accident in a hired car if you damage another vehicle or injure someone. If you think you are likely to hire a car in Thailand, make sure you obtain such extra cover from your travel agent or other insurer before departure.

Lost property
If you lose something on a bus or train, make enquiries at the local station. Most hotels and restaurants will keep lost property for a limited period of time. Or else contact the nearest local police station.

Maps
Bartholomew, Macmillan, GeoCenter, and Nelles all produce good countrywide maps of Thailand. For Bangkok try to get a map with all bus routes, as well as the *soi* (side-street) numbers, marked. The *Tour'n Guide* Map, published by SK Thaveepholcharoen, is reliable, and can

be purchased at most hotels and bookshops. Most of the free magazines distributed in the hotels also have reasonably good maps.

Free local maps are available from tourist offices and many guest houses. While the standard of cartography is not high, these maps are often very useful sources of tourist information.

Measurements and sizes
Almost everything in Thailand is metric. All distances are measured in kilometres, weights in kilos, and liquids in litres. Thailand also has one or two of its own terms. Thus, a *sok* is 0.5m (1^{1}/2ft), a *wah* is 2m (6^{1}/2ft), and a *rai* is 1,600sq m (17,220sq ft).

Media
Thailand has two English-language newspapers, *The Bangkok Post* and *The Nation,* both of which provide local and international news, and can be purchased in most big hotels and news stalls. The *Asian Wall Street Journal*, the *International Herald Tribune, Time* and *Newsweek* are also widely available.

Thailand also has some 400 radio stations broadcasting from Bangkok and the provinces. Several stations have English-language broadcasts, listed in the English-language newspapers.

Satellite television is now available in most hotels.

Money matters
The Thai currency is denominated in baht, and each baht in turn is divided into 100 satang. Thai notes consist of 1,000 baht (orange and grey), 500 baht (purple), 100 baht (red), 50 baht (blue),

20 baht (green) and 10 baht (brown). Thai coins are 25 satang, 50 satang, 1 baht, 5 baht and 10 baht. As a rule, carry small notes, as in many places it can be hard getting change for a 500 baht note.

The Thai baht is freely interchangeable with most other currencies, although outside tourist centres exchange banks are few and far between. Rates are generally advertised outside the bank or in the local newspaper.

Bank services

Local and foreign banks provide standard services nationwide. Larger towns and cities have more reliable opening times. They are open from 8.30am to 3.30pm (*Mon–Fri*), except on public and bank holidays.

Bank currency exchange offices generally operate from 8am to 9pm daily, including holidays, although quite often they have an annoying tendency to be closed when you actually need them.

Cheques and credit cards

Thomas Cook traveller's cheques, denominated in US dollars, are accepted in banks and authorised bureaux de change.

Outside of Bangkok the major hotels will happily accept your traveller's cheques, but the smaller hotels and most of the banks probably will not be able to do so.

Major international credit and charge cards, such as American Express, Diners Club, Carte Blanche, MasterCard and VISA are accepted by major banks, restaurants, hotels and shops.

If you need to transfer money quickly, you can use the MoneyGram℠ Money Transfer service. Just take some form of identification with you, and you will be able to send or receive money in minutes from over 100 countries around the world. For more details, go to your nearest Thomas Cook location, or in the UK call *Freephone 0800 897198.*

Banks in Bangkok

Bangkok Bank Ltd *333 Silom Rd.*
Tel: 0 2231 4333.
Citibank *82 Sathorn Nua Rd.*
Tel: 0 2232 2000.
Hong Kong and Shanghai Banking Corporation *968 Rama IV Rd.*
Tel: 0 2614 4000.
Kasikorn Bank *1 Soi Kasikornthai, Ratburana Rd.*
Tel: 0 2470 1122.
Siam Commercial Bank
9 Ratchadaphisek Rd.
Tel: 0 2544 1111.
Standard Chartered Bank *Sathorn Nakhon Tower, 100 Sathorn Nua Rd.*
Tel: 0 2724 4000.

Tricyles are a common sight in some parts

LANGUAGE

Thai is a highly complex language, with 44 consonants, 38 vowels, and 5 different tones. Few tourists will have the chance to learn it in a limited period, but a few words will prove useful. Men use the word *krap* at the end of certain sentences, and women use the work *ka*; these are indicated by (m) and (f) below.

NUMBERS

0	Soon	7	Jet	14	Sip-see	21	Yee-sip-et
1	Nung	8	Baet	15	Sip-ha	30	Sam-sip
2	Song	9	Gao	16	Sip-hok	100	Nung roi
3	Sam	10	Sip	17	Sip-jet	1,000	Nung pan
4	See	11	Sip-et	18	Sip-baet	10,000	Nung meun
5	Ha	12	Sip-song	19	Sip-gao		
6	Hok	13	Sip-sam	20	Yee-sip		

BASIC PHRASES

Thank you	Kop khun krap(m)/ka(f)
Hello/goodbye	Sawatdee krap(m)/ka(f)
Yes	Chai or krap(m)/ka(f)
No	Mai
How are you?	Sabai dee reu?
I'm fine	Sabai dee
I'm not well	Mai sabai krap(m)/ka(f)
Never mind	Mai pen rai
I understand	Kao chai
I don't understand	Mai kao chai
Please speak slowly	Prot puut cha-cha
I'm sorry	Sia chai
Excuse me	Kor thot
Very good	Dee maak
No good	Mai dee
Cheap	Took
Too expensive	Paeng pai
Too small	Lek pai
Too big	Yai pai
A little	Nid noi

QUESTIONS

What is your name?	Khun chu arai?
My name is...	Pom chu... (male)
	Chan chu... (female)
How old are you?	Ayu taorai?
I am (ten) years old	Ayu (sip) pi

Do you have...?	Mi mai...?
Where is the hotel?	Rongraem yu tinai?
What is this in Thai?	Thai riak wa arai?
How much is this?	Nee taorai?

DIRECTIONS

Where are you going?	Pai nai?
I'm going to...	Ja pai...
Where is the...?	Yu tii nai...?
Turn right	Lieo khwa
Turn left	Lieo sai
Straight on	Trong pai
Stop here	Jop tinni

PLACES

Airport	Sanambin
Bank	Tanakaan
Bathroom	Hong nam
Beach	Hat
Bus station	Sa-tanee rot meh
Embassy	Sa-tantoot
Hospital	Rong payabaan
Hotel	Rong raem
Island	Ko
Market	Talaht

Police station	Satanee tamruat	**Prawns**	Kung
Police	Tamruat	**Rice**	Khao
Post office	Prai-sanee	**Fried rice**	Khao pat
Railway station	Satanee rot fai	**Curry**	Kaeng
Restaurant	Raan ahaan	**Seafood**	Aahaan thaleh
River	Maenam	**Steamed crab**	(Kam) pu nung
Street	Thanon	**(claws)**	
Side-street/lane	Soi	**Mixed vegetables**	Pat Pak
Train	Rot fai	**Thai spicy salad**	Yam
Town	Meung	**Lobster**	Gung mangkorn
		Eggs	Khai
TRANSPORT		**Plain omelette**	Khai jiao
Boat	Reuah	**Black pepper**	Phrik thai
Air-con bus	Rot tour	**Salt**	Kleua
Car	Rot keng	**Hot (spicy)**	Pet
Dangerous	Antarai	**Not hot**	Mai pet
Motorbike	Rot motorcye	**Delicious**	Aroy
Please drive slowly	Prot kap rot cha cha	**I can't eat...**	Kin... mai dai
Petrol	Nam man	**I'm vegetarian**	Kin jeh
I have no petrol	Namman mot leo		
It doesn't work	Mai tit	**FRUIT**	
Garage	Rong rot	**Banana**	Kluai
Help	Chuay pom (m)	**Coconut**	Maphrao-on
	Chuay diichan (f)	**Lime**	Manao
		Mango	Ma muang
TIME		**Orange**	Som
Today	Wan nee	**Papaya**	Malako
Tomorrow	Proong nee	**Pineapple**	Sapparot
Yesterday	Meua wan nee	**Watermelon**	Taeng moh
This week	Atit ni		
Next week	Atit na	**DRINK**	
This month	Deuan ni	**Water**	Nam
Next month	Deuan na	**A glass of water**	Nam plao
Now	Dio nee	**Tea**	Chaa
Later	Tee lang	**Coffee**	Cafee
Minute	Na tee	**No sugar**	Mai sai nam-taan
Hour	Chua mong		
How many hours?	Kee chua mong?		
FOOD			
Beef	Neua		
Chicken	Gai	The fine face of	
Duck	Phet	a Phang Nga	
Fish	Pla	fisherman	
Pork	Moo		

The fine face of a Phang Nga fisherman

National holidays

Thai public holidays vary from year to year according to the lunar calendar. Always check with the tourist authority or embassy. During Songkran (April), the Thai New Year, hotels in Chiang Mai, Hua Hin, Pattaya and Phuket tend to be booked weeks ahead, and it can be difficult getting transport to and from Bangkok. Restaurants, cinemas and nightclubs generally remain open.

1 January New Year's Day
Late January Chinese New Year's Day
Early March Makha Bucha Day
6 April Chakri Day
12–14 April Songkran
1 May National Labour Day
5 May Coronation Day
Late April/early May Royal Ploughing Ceremony
May–June Visakha Puja Day
Late July Asalha Puja Day
Late July Khao Phansa
12 August The Queen's Birthday
23 October Chulalongkorn Day
5 December The King's Birthday
10 December Constitution Day
31 December New Year's Eve

Opening hours

Most commercial organisations in Bangkok operate five days a week. Government offices are open Monday to Friday from 8.30am to 4.30pm (some close for one hour for lunch), and banks from 8.30am to 3.30pm. Supermarkets and department stores are generally open daily from 10am to 7pm.

Museums normally open from Wednesday to Sunday, being closed on Monday, Tuesday and holidays. It is well worth checking first.

Conversion Table

FROM	TO	MULTIPLY BY
Inches	Centimetres	2.54
Feet	Metres	0.3048
Yards	Metres	0.9144
Miles	Kilometres	1.6090
Acres	Hectares	0.4047
Gallons	Litres	4.5460
Ounces	Grams	28.35
Pounds	Grams	453.6
Pounds	Kilograms	0.4536
Tons	Tonnes	1.0160

To convert back, for example from centimetres to inches, divide by the number in the third column.

Men's Suits

UK		36	38	40	42	44	46	48
Thailand & Rest of Europe	46	48	50	52	54	56	58
USA		36	38	40	42	44	46	48

Dress Sizes

UK		8	10	12	14	16	18
France		36	38	40	42	44	46
Italy		38	40	42	44	46	48
Thailand & Rest of Europe		34	36	38	40	42	44
USA		6	8	10	12	14	16

Men's Shirts

UK	14	14.5	15	15.5	16	16.5	17
Thailand & Rest of Europe	36	37	38	39/40	41	42	43
USA	14	14.5	15	15.5	16	16.5	17

Men's Shoes

UK	7	7.5	8.5		9.5	10.5	11
Thailand & Rest of Europe	41	42	43		44	45	46
USA	8	8.5	9.5	10.5	11.5	12

Women's Shoes

UK	4.5		5	5.5		6	6.5	7
Thailand & Rest of Europe	38	38.5	39			40	41
USA		6	6.5	7	7.5		8	8.5

Organised tours

Tour operators around the world offer a wide choice of package tours to Thailand. These can range from three-day trips (as part of a three-centre tour taking in Hong Kong and Singapore), to thirty days, and include all air transport, transfers, accommodation and sightseeing. Thomas Cook, Abercrombie and Kent, Jetset Tours and Trailfinders are all rated among the leaders.

Local organised tours can also be arranged for almost any and every destination. Make sure you use a reputable organisation. Unauthorised guides and people who approach you on the streets are to be avoided at all costs.

The following agents in Bangkok are recommended by the Tourist Authority of Thailand (TAT).

Diethelm Travel *Kian Gwan II Building, 140/1 Wireless Rd. Tel: 0 2255 9150; www.diethelmtravel.com*

Overseas International Travel Service *21st Floor, Rajathevee Tower, 77/283 Phayathai Rd. Tel: 0 2653 9050.*

Ultima Travel *Judis Tower, 21/53, 3rd Floor Soi 19, Petch Buri Rd. Tel: 0 2254 6078; www.ultima.co.th*

World Travel Service *1053 Charoen Krung Rd. Tel: 0 2233 5900. www.wts-thailand.com*

Pharmacies

Pharmacies are found in all the main towns. They sell almost everything that a normal pharmacy at home does, from medicinal drugs to contraceptives, and everything to do with personal hygiene. Prescriptions are not generally needed for medicinal drugs, but they are often sold under different brands, so bring the generic name. Always check the expiry dates before purchasing.

Photography

Film is widely available in Thailand, although, just to be sure, most visitors prefer to bring film with them. Keen photographers should also bring a polarising lens to reduce the glare, and bags of silicate chips to stop moisture getting into the camera.

Most international film manufacturers have local finishing laboratories that offer marginally cheaper rates than back home.

Places of worship

Christian churches are found in Bangkok and several provincial capitals. Services are mainly in Thai, with occasional services in English, French or German.

In Bangkok

Assumption Cathedral (Roman Catholic) *23 Oriental Ave. Tel: 0 2234 8556.*

Christ Church *11 Convent Rd. Tel: 0 2233 8525.*

ต้อนรับเฉพาะสุภาพชนเท่านั้น

POLITE PEOPLE ARE INVITED

To do what, we wonder?

The Evangelical Church *end of Soi 10, Sukhumvit Rd. Tel: 0 2251 9539.*
Holy Redeemer Catholic Church *123/19 Soi Raum Rudee, Wireless (Witthayu) Rd. Tel: 0 2256 6305.*

Police

In case of trouble, contact the tourist police. They generally speak English and can be recognised by their badges. The main office is in **Bangkok** (*tel: 1699 in emergencies,* or *0 2678 6800*). The tourist police also have offices in **Chiang Mai** (*tel: 0 5324 8130*), **Hat Yai** (*tel: 0 7424 6733*), **Kanchana Buri** (*tel: 0 3451 2795*), **Pattaya** (*tel: 0 3842 5937*), **Phuket** (*tel: 0 7621 9878*) and **Surat Thani** (*tel: 0 7742 1281*).

Post offices

Almost every town has a post office. Big towns also have *poste restante* offices which receive mail from abroad and have international telephone and fax services.

Airmail generally takes five or six days to reach Europe, and eight or nine days to the United States. Packages can also be sent home by air or ship, although you will have to present the contents for inspection at the customs window.

The General Post Office (GPO) has its head office on Charoen Krung Road in Bangkok and is open from 8am–8pm (*Mon–Fri*), and 9am–1pm (*Sat, Sun and public holidays*). Outside Bangkok, offices are open 8.30am–4.30pm (*Mon–Fri*), and 9am–1pm (*Sat*).

Public transport

By air

Thai Airways or its associates operates daily flights between Bangkok and virtually every major town in Thailand. Bangkok Airways also has flights from Bangkok to Ko Samui and from Phuket to Ko Samui.

Reservations can be made through any authorised Thai Inter Travel Agent. Thai Airways main office is on *6 Lan Luang Road* (*tel: 0 2280 0060*). Book well in advance at all times and especially over local holidays when seats are taken up months ahead.

The local airport tax is 30 baht. Planes leave from Don Muang Domestic Airport next to the international terminal.

By bus

Buses offer a fast, if somewhat harrowing, means of transport to most places. VIP tour coaches offer greater comfort but at a slightly higher cost. Normal public buses are designed for Thais, not foreigners, and leg room is limited.

A number of private companies also run air-conditioned and VIP coaches to major tourist destinations. Bangkok has the following public bus terminals.
Eastern Bus Terminal *Sukhumvit Rd. Tel: 0 2392 9227* or *0 2391 9829.*
Northern and Northeastern Bus Terminal *Kampangphet Rd. Tel: 0 2272 5242.*
Southern Bus Terminal *Phra Pinklao Rd, Thonburi. Tel: 0 2434 5557.*

By rail

A slow, but efficient, rail system links major northern, northeastern and southern towns with the capital. Trains from Bangkok take 12 hours to Chiang Mai, 11 hours to Nong Khai, and 12 hours to Surat Thani (the jump-off point for Ko Samui). Local trains generally have three classes. On longer trips you can also book a sleeper. Try to make reservations several days before you travel.

The main railway station in Bangkok is Hualamphong (*Rama IV Rd, tel: 0 2225 0300, ext 5200–3*) which also has a booking office for advance reservations. Most travel agents will also book train tickets at a small surcharge.

The **Visit Thailand Rail Pass** is available to visitors with international passports for travel on all State Railway of Thailand trains. It is obtainable from the advance booking office at Bangkok, Hualumphong, and other major stations, but check how worthwhile it will be.

Details of local rail, bus and ferry services are shown in the *Thomas Cook Overseas Timetable* which is available from Thomas Cook branches in the UK or by telephoning *001 44 1733 416477*.

By river
Thailand has an extensive network of waterways. In Bangkok, ferry services are the best way to avoid the traffic. The public Chao Phraya express boat costs about 20 baht, and the private long-tailed boats about 350 baht an hour.

Local transport
Meter taxis, *tuk tuks* (three-wheeled scooters), *songthaews* (pick-up truck-taxis) and tricycles operate in various parts of Thailand for most times of day or night. To avoid problems, get your hotel to write your destination down in Thai and present it to the driver. Always agree on a price before starting and remember to bargain. If one sounds too

expensive, wait for another, or take a metered taxi.

Big hotels also run their own taxis and limousines that can be rented by the hour or by the day. These are much more expensive, but generally have the advantage of an English-speaking driver.

Local buses
Buses around Bangkok are cheap and frequent, they leave extremely regularly and serve all parts of the city. More comfortable and less crowded air-conditioned buses also operate, although they cost slightly more. To work out which bus to take, it is essential to buy a map marked with bus routes. The new skytrain is fast, efficient and easy to use.

Student and youth travel
Student discounts are occasionally offered on air tickets but not on trains

Cathedral of the Assumption, Bangkok

or buses. Some museums also offer discounts, although you will need identification. There are no official youth hostels in Thailand, but the **YMCA** and **YWCA** in Bangkok offer good standards and services.
YMCA *Collins International House, 27 Sathorn Tai Rd. Tel: 0 2677 6240/5.*

Sustainable tourism
Thomas Cook is a strong advocate of ethical and fairly traded tourism and believes that the travel experience should be as good for the places visited as it is for the people who visit them. That's why we firmly support The Travel Foundation: a charity that develops solutions to help improve and protect holiday destinations, their environment, traditions and culture. To find out what you can do to make a positive difference to the places you travel to and the people who live there, please visit *www.thetravelfoundation.org.uk*

Telephones
Local and international telephone services are available in most hotels and post offices. Do not expect perfection. Because of the time differences, it can be difficult getting a line to Europe in the late afternoon.

Local phone boxes take small 1 baht, 5 baht or 10 baht coins, which have to be inserted before you dial the number.

The Thomas Cook Traveltalk card is an international pre-paid telephone card supported by 24-hour multilingual customer service. Available from Thomas Cook branches in the UK in £10 and £20 denominations, the card can be recharged by calling the customer service unit and quoting your credit card number.

Local directory assistance *13*
Domestic long distance *101*
International assistance *100*

International codes

Australia *61*	**Canada** *1*
Ireland *353*	**New Zealand** *64*
UK *44*	**USA** *1*

Time
Thailand is 7 hours ahead of Greenwich Mean Time (GMT). So, when it is noon in Bangkok, it is 5am in London, mid-night in New York and 3pm in Sydney.

Tipping
Tipping, once rarely expected, is on the increase. In some international restaurants, a 10 per cent service charge is included. In other big restaurants, tip in the region of 5 to 10 per cent – and in smaller restaurants a 20-baht note is normally adequate. It is not necessary to tip taxi drivers or cinema attendants.

Toilets
In the cities and in the tourist-visited areas, there are normally sit-down loos. In the provinces, it's squat loos, and in really far-flung provinces, a rice paddy.

If you are caught short, go into a shop or restaurant and ask for the *hong nam* (bathroom) and, to be on the safe side, always bring a toilet roll with you on your travels.

Tourist offices
Tourist information is available at Tourist Authority of Thailand (TAT) offices throughout Thailand and in certain countries abroad. The officials

are generally extremely helpful and speak English. They will distribute maps, brochures and useful information on tours, shopping, dining and, crucially, accommodation.

Bangkok
Head Office *Ratchadapisek Rd.*
Tel: 0 2694 1222; www.tourismthailand.org
Second Office *Ratchadamneon Nok Ave.*
Tel: 0 2282 9773.

Chiang Mai
105/1 Chiang Mai-Lamphun Rd.
Tel: 0 5324 8604; tatchmai@or.th

Hat Yai
1/1 Soi 2 Niphat Uthit 3 Rd.
Tel: 0 7424 3747; tatsgkhi@tat.or.th

Kanchana Buri
Saeng Chuto Rd.
Tel: 0 3457 7200; tatkan@tat.or.th

Nakhon Ratchasima
2102/2104 Mittraphap Rd.
Tel: 0 4421 3666; tatsima@tat.or.th

Pattaya
382/1 Mu 10 Chaihat Rd.
Tel: 0 3842 7667; tatchon@tat.or.th

Phitsanulok
209/7–8 Surasi Trade Centre.
Tel: 0 55253 1063; tatphlok@tat.or.th

Phuket
73-75 Phuket Rd.
Tel: 0 7621 1036; tatphket@tat.or.th

Surat Thani
5 Talat Mai Rd, Ban Don.
Tel: 0 7728 8818; tatsurat@tat.or.th

Ubon Ratchathani
264/1 Khaun Thani Rd.
Tel: 0 4524 3770; tatubon@tat.or.th

Don Muang International Airport, Bangkok

Thomas Cook offices
Turismo Thai is the Thomas Cook Network Worldwide Licensee in Thailand. The main branch is at:

Turismo Thai Building *511 Soi 6, Sri Ayutthaya Rd, Bangkok 10400.*
Tel: 0 2245 1551; fax 0 2246 3993.

Besides offering a full leisure travel service, they also organise airport transfers, rail tickets and reservations, car hire, and give general information and assistance.

They can provide emergency assistance in the event of loss or theft of Thomas Cook traveller's cheques.

Travellers with disabilities
Few special facilities exist for travellers with disabilities in Thailand. Lift services are, however, available in all the major hotels, and wheelchairs are available at Don Muang International Airport, and at all the local airports.

The Tourist Authority of Thailand (TAT) or Thai embassies abroad should be able to provide information prior to arrival. There is also the Association for the Disabled in Bangkok (*tel: 0 2463 5929*).

Valeting/laundry
Most hotels will offer their guests a fast and efficient laundry service. Most items are returned the same day if they are given in before 9am, and if you are in a real hurry they can be laundered and returned in as little as four hours. Prices will vary depending on the quality of the establishment, but are invariably cheaper than in Western hotels.

ACKNOWLEDGEMENTS
Thomas Cook Publishing wishes to thank the following libraries and associations for their assistance in the preparation of this book.

DAVID HENLEY/CPA MEDIA 1, 2, 5b, 6, 7, 11a, 11b, 12, 13, 14, 16, 17, 18, 19, 21, 23, 29, 31, 33a, 33b, 35, 39, 40, 42b, 47b, 49, 51c, 53, 59, 61b, 63b, 65, 71, 72, 78, 79, 84a, 86, 87, 88b, 90, 91, 96, 97, 103, 104, 105, 106a, 108, 109, 111, 112, 116, 118, 119, 122, 123, 124, 125a, 125b, 125c, 127, 130, 132, 133a, 133b, 135a, 135b, 138a, 139b, 140, 141, 142, 143, 144, 145, 146, 150, 151a, 151b, 154, 158, 159, 160, 161, 164, 165, 166, 170, 171, 172, 173, 189, 190

PICTURES COLOUR LIBRARY 44

The remaining pictures are held in the AA Photo Library and were taken by RICK STRANGE.

Proofreading: JOANNE OSBORN for CAMBRIDGE PUBLISHING MANAGEMENT LIMITED

Send your thoughts to
books@thomascook.com

We're committed to providing the very best up-to-date information in our travel guides and constantly strive to make them as useful as they can be. You can help us to improve future editions by letting us have your feedback. If you've made a wonderful discovery on your travels that we don't already feature, if you'd like to inform us about recent changes to anything that we do include, or if you simply want to let us know your thoughts about this guidebook and how we can make it even better – we'd love to hear from you.

Send us ideas, discoveries and recommendations today and then look out for your valuable input in the next edition of this title. And, as an extra 'thank you' from Thomas Cook Publishing, you'll be automatically entered into our exciting monthly prize draw.

Emails to the above address, or letters to Travellers Project Editor, Thomas Cook Publishing, PO Box 227, Unit 18, Coningsby Road, Peterborough PE3 8SB, UK.

Please don't forget to let us know which title your feedback refers to!